# MONEY MASTERING

The Simplest, Yet Most Important Money Management Tips You Should Have Been Taught at School

ILIYANA STAREVA
FHRAM CARLOS DIAZ OTOYA

Copyright © 2022 by Iliyana Stareva & Fhram Carlos Diaz Otoya.

All rights reserved. No part of this book may be used, reproduced or transmitted in any form or by any means, electronic or mechanical, including photocopy, recording or any information storage and retrieval system, without prior permission in writing from the authors except in the case of brief quotations in critical articles or reviews.

First edition 5 September 2022.
Cover design by Aleksandra Stareva.
Independently published in the Netherlands.

For more information, or to book an event, contact Iliyana Stareva:
iliyana.stareva@gmail.com
http://www.iliyanastareva.com/
**ISBN: 9798351133966**

# DEDICATION

To our beautiful daughter – may you never have money issues and if you ever do, let this be your guide in addition to everything we will teach you and have been teaching you already!

# CONTENTS

ACKNOWLEDGMENTS .......................................................... I
CHAPTER 1 INTRODUCTION ................................................ 1
CHAPTER 2 MONEY MANAGEMENT TODAY AND WHY IT MATTERS .................................................................. 7
CHAPTER 3 BLUEPRINT FOR EFFECTIVE MONEY MANAGEMENT ............................................................... 23
CHAPTER 4 CREATING AND MANAGING A BUDGET ................................................................................... 35
CHAPTER 5 BUILDING AN EMERGENCY FUND ......... 57
CHAPTER 6 TACKLING DEBT ............................................ 69
CHAPTER 7 GROWING YOUR SAVINGS ....................... 85
CHAPTER 8 INVESTING ...................................................... 99
CHAPTER 9 GETTING READY FOR RETIREMENT ... 117
CHAPTER 10 SUMMARY .................................................. 127
BONUS CHAPTER THE MONEY MASTERING CHALLENGE ........................................................................ 137
ABOUT THE AUTHORS ..................................................... 143
SUPPORT THE BOOK ......................................................... 145
REFERENCES ........................................................................ 147

# ACKNOWLEDGMENTS

To our families and friends for the support and ideas while writing this book. Special thanks to Iliyana's sister – Aleksandra Stareva – for designing the cover of the book.

# CHAPTER 1
# INTRODUCTION

Five years ago, we met salsa dancing in a bar in Dublin, Ireland.

You didn't expect a money book to start this way, did you? But this is how our story began which led to this book.

We have both had some difficult and hardworking times. We have both been expats for dozens of years now – alone and far away from our families. Each of us had to start from zero after the initial push and support of our families to leave our home countries in the search of a better future. That experience had us learn a ton but also work very hard. We have both had dealings with figuring out how to make life work with the little money we were individually earning when starting. We have both had to deal with debt and get out of difficult situations, not knowing the best way out and stressing along the way while researching on our own what to do. We have also both had our successes over the years through lots of mistakes that helped us learn. Life saw us both living in different countries before one unexpected night we met thanks to a joint passion of ours – salsa dancing. At that time, we had individually already built a relatively stable financial basis after years of working and when we got together, joining forces made it more powerful. We started dreaming about what we could achieve and by bouncing off ideas of how we could do it, dreams began to come true much more quickly together.

After years of hard work, some savings and some successes in the stock market, we now look back and realise that through a lot of bumps, we've managed to achieve our biggest dream – have a

INTRODUCTION

family, living in our own house in the country we wanted to be, being able to travel as we please and enjoy ourselves.

And when we look back, what pushed us to get here was a conversation we had in the morning after we got engaged. At that stage, everything we had done and achieved we had done thanks to a lot of hard work and a lot of research on our own in terms of how to deal with certain money situations. We spoke about how we viewed money and what we had done with it in the past and what we were doing with it now. We realised we were doing well but we could do better in terms of allocating our finances in a more structured way and finding ways for additional income. We started to dream about what was possible. We started to talk about our goals and hopes for the future and this time we decided to put a plan together not just talk about it. But we wanted to make the plan very clear and actionable, backed up by best practices. We started intensively reading about the topic of managing money, investing, saving, etc. We listened to webinars and watched YouTube videos. We spoke to friends and family. We realised there's a whole other world out there when it comes to making money, managing it, and growing it. There was so much we didn't know, including some basic things. We also realised that a lot of friends or family members didn't know either.

There is no education out there on managing personal finances. Few parents teach their children. A course on this does not exist in schools and universities. We didn't get into this with the idea to write a book about managing your money well. We made smart management of personal finances a very natural part of our daily lives as we got more and more curious about the topic.

This book became the outcome of our deep dive into money over the last few years. Everything you will read on these pages is based on a ton of research, conversations with friends, family, and colleagues and especially on our own experiences and learnings. Most importantly, this book is based on our own story, not on suppositions or ideas.

Are we financial gurus? No, although we've researched the topic of personal finances so much.

Do we have degrees in Finance? No, although one of us did study Finance in Business school but Finance about how to run a business rather than personal finances.

Do we not worry about our financial future? Of course we do, especially because we have a family but we don't worry as much about it as we used to before knowing what we know now.

Are we quitting our day-to-day jobs knowing all this? No, we both love our day-to-day jobs. It's our choice to stay.

Are we millionaires? No, but we live comfortably, enjoying life the way we want to.

Do we have our future secured? We'd like to think so, especially with certain steps we've taken that you'll learn about in this book. But you never know so plans B and C are always important.

We wrote this book for people who want to live a life where you control your money instead of them controlling you. We wrote to help you with advice on how to live comfortably and secure a better future. We wrote it because we believe that there are two fronts in life – enjoying it now and not sacrificing the joys presented to you, but also preparing for the future in a way that's sustainable and doesn't make you live frugally.

Our goal is not to ask you to sacrifice everything. We don't want you to work to perfection. Life happens. Not every week and month and year are going to be the same. Sometimes we

## INTRODUCTION

spend more than planned because we decided to enjoy and build memories now. But we do that without worrying because we've planned for the rest.

This is not a book that's going to make you a millionaire. Our goal is not to give you advice on how to get rich. The internet is full of articles, videos and courses saying that getting rich is easy, suggesting simple steps to financial freedom tomorrow. We don't believe in those, it's a dream. Is it possible? Maybe but not in our experience. It also goes back to what rich means to you. Like anything, acquiring wealth requires time and effort. It doesn't happen overnight.

This book was written for the ordinary person like you and us. It's easy and simple to understand. It's different from most other books out there. We've read so many of them while working on this book. Most books either sell an unrealistic dream about becoming a millionaire tomorrow or are way too detailed with too many calculations and too many steps that overwhelm a regular person. This is a book for the ordinary person looking for some guidance and practical, easy-to-apply tips every day. This is basic financial literacy that no one is teaching you at school. We aim to provide you with a simple system to master your money daily, with a guide that allows you to be fully in control of your money instead of them controlling you.

If you're already managing your personal finances well and have accumulated savings and investments, then this book might be simple for you. You would still get new tips and tricks, but this book is really for those who are only now consciously thinking about how they manage their money and want to be better. Those who want a more manageable approach to personal finances that allows you to live a good life with strategies for the short, mid, and long term. Those who want to tackle debt and focus on better controlling their finances to be able to save and invest for the future.

Disclaimer: We're not certified financial advisors and this book does not provide any type of personalised financial advice based on your individual needs as a reader. This book is not a guarantee for any financial success or gains and does not consider your individual circumstances. Our goal is to teach you some basics when it comes to money and how you manage it. The book contains tips and tricks based on our experience, research, and knowledge. The advice given is for educational purposes only and should not be relied upon to make financial, investment or savings decisions. Depending on your situation, especially if it's complicated, you can always hire a financial advisor who can provide professional help. And so we get this out of the way, we – the authors – cannot be held responsible for any action or claim resulting from the use of this book or the decisions that you make. Ultimately, everything depends on you, the research that you do, how you manage your money and whether and how you decide to save and/or invest it. It's solely your responsibility.

And if after reading our book you want to keep in touch and keep getting helpful materials, go to www.iliyanastareva.com to explore the Money Mastering section and category on the blog.

We're on a mission to help you manage your money better. Here's how this book will help you do that and what to expect from the chapters.

First, there are only 10 chapters (including the Introduction) unlike many other personal finance books that have too much information in them. Our goal is to keep it simple and focused because that's how you make a change – by doing a few things right rather than trying to do many things at once. You can jump

# INTRODUCTION

to whichever chapter you want but they build up on each other for a reason.

Chapter 2 covers why many people struggle with managing their money well and the situations they get into, whether based on bad habits or outside forces like the economy or various crises.

Chapter 3 shares our system for effective money management – we call it a blueprint.

Chapter 4 is all about budget management – how you create one, how you journal spending, and how you plan and execute around your budget.

Chapter 5 explains why you need an emergency fund and how you go about getting one.

Chapter 6 talks about debt and how you manage it better.

Chapter 7 is all about savings – how, when, and why.

Chapter 8 is about investments, what types there are, and why they matter, and we especially focus on the stock market.

Chapter 9 is about your future planning and retirement with tips based on your specific age bracket.

Chapter 10 is a summary of everything including the key focus areas.

The last chapter is a bonus and is your headstart to effective money management with a 4-week challenge we'd love you to take on as the practical implementation of this book.

Now, are you ready to start your money mastering journey?

# CHAPTER 2
# MONEY MANAGEMENT TODAY AND WHY IT MATTERS

We live in a world of constant consumerism. We spend money all the time. Sometimes for good reasons, other times because we don't have a choice (like paying bills), and at times because it's become an addiction.

Spending is like calories. The more calories you eat for the wrong reasons, the deeper you sink into bad habits that lead to bad health. In the same way, excessive spending for bad reasons will pull you deeper into the pit of debt which creates financial problems and increases stress. The deeper you sink into tough financial situations, the more unmanageable they become, and many people see no way out of it.

Statistically, only 30% of the world's population manages their finances effectively. 70% of us fail to manage our money effectively[i].

In this chapter, we'll look at the state of money management today and why it's important for regular people like you and me.

### The What

When it comes to managing money, few of us have proper financial literacy. Millennials have become better, but even they have a long way to go. Only 24% of them have some basic financial literacy[ii].

Unless our parents teach us how to deal with money (or you have a Finance career), nobody gives us a manual on how to manage it. There are no courses at school or university. Unless you actively research the topic and learn from your mistakes, you are left out in the dark, and many people never learn some basic money management fundamentals. This is why a lot of us face tough financial situations.

Not everyone aspires to be rich because not everyone is built to climb the financial success ladder or not everyone wants to climb it. However, the reality is that we all need to be able to meet our monthly financial commitments and ideally, this should be done without sleepless nights spent wondering how we're going to break even. When we reach adulthood and enter the working world, many of us go in not having the knowledge of managing money. This is the first step to financial ruin because before we know it, we find ourselves encountering various financial difficulties due to easy access to credit after employment.

To us, it's crazy that we're taught so many things at school but the lessons taught do not involve anything about learning some strategic methods to effectively manage personal finances – a skill you need every single day of your life. So, it stands to reason that facing financial woes is an all-too-common problem for many of us as we are not equipped with the money dos and don'ts from the get-go.

Also, we all grow up in different families which is our first learning ground when it comes to money management, so we adapt the good and bad habits we see through the years. It's not to blame our parents as we are all responsible for our own decisions as adults but not repeating the bad habits that we are inclined to will also aid in helping the next generation to be better at money.

And because most of us have basically never been taught how to manage our finances, we don't recognise the warning signs when problems start to arise. Even if and when some of us do, we don't know how to prevent the inevitable downward spiral when the spending frenzy begins because it's like an addiction. By nature, many of us don't like restrictions or being told how to spend money that we have worked for. Whether we are made aware of our irresponsible financial behaviours and given advice about our financial decisions, we are not very likely to follow it. Because people learn best when they make mistakes and make their own conclusions from them. But by then, certain unhealthy decisions like too many calories can severely affect your financial status and put you in a tough situation that might take you years to get out of. The simplest but most common one among ordinary people is the stress of simply making the month with what you earn and not going into debt. And when you go into debt once, it's highly likely that this will repeat month over month.

Let's look at some of the most common financial problems people get into.

## Financial mismanagement

Lots of people make poor financial choices repeatedly and get themselves into an unhealthy spending lifestyle. This happens for various reasons – wanting to look rich to keep up with friends and appearances, thinking too much about the now versus then, abusing credit cards, not knowing your finances, too much debt to deal with at the same time etc. The only way of reversing this situation is to change our spending habits. Facing personal financial woes unrelated to loss of income and earning potential is so common. Most of the time it's about spending on things you don't need, being too spontaneous or living a lifestyle way above your means just so you can fit with your social circle or present a different picture of yourself and your life to others.

Many people don't spend time examining what's got them into their current spending lifestyle. They don't ask themselves honest questions about how and why they spend or what they spend for. Financial woes don't happen overnight. They are the result of a long line of blind spending habits that lead to unhealthy distress. It's a vicious circle that many don't know how to get out of. Most of the time they don't even realise the gravity of the issue until something serious happens. Then they want to fix things immediately, but the reality is that changing this type of lifecycle requires a plan that is realistic, manageable, sustainable, and achievable on an ongoing basis. Where most people falter is putting too much pressure on themselves and setting unrealistic goals. You need to remind yourself that you did not reach an unhealthy financial state overnight, therefore the problem cannot be solved in the blink of an eye. You need to realise and accept that this is a journey. The process through it is not meant to punish you but instead to change the way you view your finances and how you manage the money you have available to you.

**Loss of income**

We live in unprecedented times and loss of income is a contributing factor to a downward spiral involving stress, particularly when it comes to those who live from paycheck to paycheck.

Loss of income could include various things – losing your job or savings for various reasons, going bankrupt if you have your own business etc. You could find yourself in a position of a serious illness, as experienced in recent times by many because of the COVID-19 pandemic, which forced people into taking extended sick leave exceeding the allowance allocated for it. For many, this resulted in unpaid leave days and basically no money coming in.

The economy can also adversely affect income in times when there is a severe economic crisis. This is when companies are forced to reduce staff and either give them shorter working hours or resort to retrenchments, resulting in a direct loss of income because inevitably, salaries are adjusted accordingly or eliminated. Just listen to the news now and you'll hear so much about layoffs that people were simply not prepared for.

If we look at other present-day occurrences, the current conflict between Ukraine and Russia has a direct impact on the entire world. Hikes in food prices, energy bills, and the overall cost of daily living has shot through the roof in a matter of months. Inflation is at an all-time hight. We used to buy a kilo of chicken for €5.50 just five months ago, now it's €9.50. A situation like this can occur at any time in our lives and no matter how far away we are from it physically, we live in a world that's much more connected than before, and the effects are felt everywhere. For some who were barely managing to get by before this war, imagine how they are enduring the price hikes at present? Without savings or another source of income to fall back on, the days ahead would look bleak, adding more strain to an already fragile financial situation.

Any form of income loss puts us in a difficult financial position trying to figure out how to solve to issue when we simply don't have money. Most people are not prepared for situations like this. They leave it to figure it out when it happens. You're not to blame if you haven't prepared for this. For many, it's difficult to organise and plan for emergencies until they happen as you already have so much to take care of now. What you need to focus on here is starting small and building bit by bit.

Wealthier people can be suddenly impacted by loss of income too. A severe economic crisis affects everyone equally and will be relative to all financial circumstances. The challenge is that when people think about preparing for emergencies, they think big. Especially in a difficult situation, people get stuck with the need to fix this immediately instead of being smart and patient to do it bit by bit. It's much easier to convince yourself to save €5 every day than €500 every month.

**Retail therapy**

As a society, we have come to believe that money makes us happier. This can't be further from the truth. Money enables you to either buy certain things or afford certain experiences which might make you happier. There are a ton of studies out there talking about how it's experiences and spiritual things like gratitude as well as helping others that give us a long-term boost of happiness rather than an impulsive buy of stuff. The latter which might give you a happiness boost for 30 minutes and then you forget about them. Because when you have it, it's no longer interesting, it's no longer special. But when you have memories of the last vacation to come back to, your brain automatically sends renewed feelings of joy.

Many of us use money for therapy. Overspending and unnecessary spending to help with your emotions is driven by the weakness of attractive eye candy as bait to lure individuals into a frenzy that is later regretted. This is often driven by pure advertising for people who have access to credit cards and don't think twice about the consequences of debt. Companies have huge marketing and advertising departments. Their sole role is to sell us stuff. The temptation is all around us. And with social media now, simply seeing how other people live and the things they own, makes you want the same just so you're not excluded and feel like you belong. It's so exaggerated nowadays that deciding what you truly want is really difficult so you end up spending money on stuff you actually don't want but because others have, you think you should have them as well. Most of the time, until you see an ad or someone's Instagram, you wouldn't even have thought about the thing that you now want to buy.

If you already have a spending problem, you'll know that the more you spend over time and build up debt, the more depressed you become. That depression still doesn't stop you from doing it again and again as you have built up the habit of spending over time to cure your feelings. It's a vicious circle that seems to have no end. Retail therapy is like an addiction. You think you will feel better only to realise that you've overspent on your credit card. And when buyer's remorse sets in, it's your mental health being affected as you end up guilting yourself out about the unnecessary spending. Unnecessary spending to a person facing financial difficulty is what overeating is to a person who is trying to lose weight. It reminds you that you've cheated on your financial diet and often steers you to the path of giving up the journey to financial stability.

Overspending to make you feel better is an easy trap to fall into. In the fast-paced world that we live in, we all want to acquire things easier, faster, and more conveniently, even if it costs more than what we can afford. We placate ourselves with the fact that we did it because we really needed it, not giving much thought to the consequences or our actual feelings. So instead of focusing on the problem, we try to mask it by spending, not thinking about whether we have the money or not or if we have what would be the trade-off.

When we find ourselves in the overspending category, we need to identify what is classified as overspending and the reasons behind it. People don't overspend because they consciously want to waste money. It is usually done out of bad habits and because dealing with emotions isn't easy. As anything, it takes practice and if you use money as retail therapy, you need to realise this is a problem and start working off a budget, practising daily discipline and perhaps doing lists etc. to help you manage.

**Living off credit**

Creditors have made living in debt far too easily accessible to everyone. Opening a current account is easy and the minute we're earning an income, irrespective of how menial, credit is made available to us. The worst part is that the more credit you have, the more credit you are offered because maintaining it for a short while increases your credit score. While this may seem attractive and emits a sense of worth in that you literally can purchase anything your heart desires, this credit comes at a high price and only encourages unnecessary overspending.

The actual truth is that we are so impressed by the fact that multiple creditors think us worthy of their sophisticated credit cards that we greedily grab them all. Sometimes we take advantage of the situation because we are unable to meet our monthly commitments and pay our bills. Credit cards are viewed as a saviour. But when you get your bill at the end of the month, then the truth sinks in. And when you can't pay it in full, you start accumulating interest. It becomes a life lived in a vicious circle of paying off credit card bills. Creditors are in the business of making money. They don't care about the consumer as their objective is the bottom line which is sales.

Credit cards are a bigger problem than a solution and certainly when it comes to your regular finances. Paying debt with debt is amongst the worse downfalls of living a life full of credit. Your salary will eventually become no match for the credit you've accumulated. Many people get multiple credit cards so they can rely on whichever one still has credit left. They end up repaying one for the other. But this is not your money you're spending. When you are living on credit, you are living off the bank's money and there will come a point where you need to repay that money. To many, this is a moot point, but if you're addicted to overspending or unnecessary spending, that becomes irrelevant. Most overspenders only care about having access to the funds to finance the lifestyle they desire, no matter what the cost, aside from financial, is in the long term. The only way to overcome the anxiety of not being able to pay those bills is to not put yourself in that position in the first place. It's a tough task when the bills are piling up and there just isn't enough money to pay them. This keeps the destructive circle of debt rolling because to feed one side of it, you'd have to tap into the other side by borrowing again. Although it offers immediate temporary relief, it's a short-term solution and it creates a much bigger long-term problem when you reach the stage of having to pay that loan back. Most often, people who are facing financial woes are inclined to take out personal loans as a solution to a financial issue they are facing. You need to remember that the long-term problem here is the inability to manage your finances effectively and taking out a loan to resolve existing debt is a short-term solution that will only exacerbate the long-term problem. It accumulates debt as the repayments are always at a premium interest rate which means that you are creating expensive debt.

Constant debt can make you sick. You obsess over it because you want to get rid of it as soon as possible. Instead of enjoying how you live, you spend all your time thinking about how you can make more money to get rid of debt. A valuable motto to live by is that if you didn't earn it, you shouldn't spend it. This applies especially to those with financial constraints. We use credit cards only when we cannot pay with a debit card (for example, when renting a car on a trip), but we always pay it in full the next month, we leave nothing to accumulate.

**Lack of future planning**

According to the World Economic Forum, we now live longer but are not prepared for it[iii]. Most people will outlive their savings by eight to 20 years. Read that again: 8-20 years! What does a retired person who no longer works do for 8-20 years of their life without money? Most of us are not prepared for the future because governmental retirement programs are not enough and because we don't have a plan for how to cover the gap.

If we look at state pension funds after retirement today, they're not what they used to be. The increase in the cost of daily living is not matched with the amount of state pension funds that are allocated monthly. Pension funds cannot sustain our daily demands such as medical bills, accommodation, food, and other essentials because they're simply not enough. Relying on somebody else to see to your needs when you have pensioned off will remove the independence you maintained through all the years of your life. Imagine working your whole life and earning a salary that you just about managed with and thereafter, when you retire, you end up with a small fraction of that salary in the form of a state pension. Unlike years ago, when our grandparents could live comfortably with a state pension, the young generation of today doesn't even think about how thin those funds have become. When you are no longer at employable age, making sure that you still maintain the lifestyle you have been living can only be done by investing in your financial future. Thinking about this early is important so you don't find yourself in an impossible situation where after working for so many years you can't enjoy the freedom you now have. We've heard stories of people selling all their assets (like their home) just to make do. That's a terrible situation to be in for the last years of your life.

For many of us, the thought of planning for our financial future rarely crosses our minds, regardless of whether we're talking about pensions or something else. We are so caught up with current financial demands that the mist overshadowing the future is blinding. While working for most of our lives, we all aim to live independently. However, what happens to that independence when things take a turn for the worse in the future? We all are aware of recent circumstances such as COVID that have turned our lives upside down and hindered our usual spending routines. What if a bigger disaster occurs and we find ourselves without an income and no financial means to fall back on? Without proper planning and preparation for our financial future, we would not have a solid financial ground to stand on.

Sound financial management is also about deploying easy techniques to avoid problems that are likely to arise such as lack of money after retirement or emergencies. We believe there needs to be a balance between enjoying life at present and getting ready for the future so you can enjoy then as well.

## The Why

One of the most popular terms in personal finances is "financial freedom." It can mean different things to different people. In fact, it gets confused a lot and many believe it's about becoming a millionaire. To us, financial freedom is basically getting to a lifestyle where you have enough money to live as you please. To one person, enough money might mean becoming a millionaire, to another just getting by without worries every month and to another quitting their nine to five job. Ultimately, it's the freedom that allows you a life without stress, worries, and debt so that you can pursue your wants and dreams. It gives you both time and money to spend as you please, ideally leading to a secure future. It allows you to be independent to easily sustain the lifestyle you want without having to rely on others. Having financial security in your future is a decision that only you can make. It takes strategic management of your current finances. Financial freedom is the reward you receive for hard and consistent work and diligence with money that leads to achieved goals and dreams.

It's no secret that financial well-being is directly related to mental health. As soon as there are financial issues, it tends to have a significant impact on our emotional well-being. The stress and worry of not being able to pay bills, provide for yourself and your family, or even have a simple coffee date with your friends can cause untold damage to a person's sense of worth. Struggling to make ends meet from day to day because of mismanaging finances only adds to your load of worries. It really doesn't matter whether you earn a menial salary or an extravagant one. The thought of not being able to put food on the table or struggling to get through the month with exhausted funds because of too much debt is coupled with sleepless nights and loss of concentration even when you're awake. Stress over finances also puts our hopes, dreams, and goals at the back of the shelf as concentration on what should be given priority and dealt with is completely lost. Not making ends meet accelerates anxiety and puts us in distress, hence we tap into our credit cards and max our overdraft amount blindly adding more fuel to the fire.

Most of us are powered by the need to survive in life without the specific knowledge of how it should be done. Surviving life and its misfortunes has become increasingly difficult as life isn't as simplified as it was a century ago. Some of us are fortunate enough to have been taught by our parents that being financially free is important if you want to live a good life. But knowing it's important is not the same as knowing how to get there.

There are various perks and benefits to financial freedom and financial literacy:

- It minimises the level of stress faced from financial mismanagement which ultimately contributes to a healthy mind. Financial stress is known to be one of the most significant contributing factors to several mental health conditions caused by mismanagement and mounting debt.

- It can impact your relationship positively. Couples who have adopted a specific solid financial plan do not incur unnecessary stress and relationship problems as often. Working together toward a healthy financial future usually builds stronger and more fulfilled relationships.

- It offers more options to enjoy a fulfilled life at your own leisure. People who manage their money well and plan how they are going to spend or invest it have better control over their finances. They can be a lot more flexible with their budgets than when finances are tied up in debt.

- It gives you more freedom to choose how you spend your time. Whether you still work for someone else or yourself, by managing your finances well, you're much better able to control what you do outside of your working hours.

- It allows for rainy days, unexpected surprises, or emergencies. When you have savings to fall back on, should something more extreme happen, you can face it calmly with a solution already there.

- It gives you leeway to offer generosity and help others. There's nothing more rewarding than the ability to offer a hand to those who truly need it, whether that's in the form of money or your time.

People who have good personal finance management strategies possess the power to carry a positive effect on young children. By teaching them the importance of financial management from an early age, they have a chance of being amongst the 30% who effectively manage their money. People with sound management of their personal finances usually have children who are more likely to become financially stable in adulthood resulting from what they had seen, heard, and learned while growing up.

Managing your money well takes discipline, drive and determination. Becoming financially free, financially independent or simply acquiring better financial literacy is not going to happen overnight. It requires planning and change of habits.

## The How

So, what is the solution to not being a part of the 70% who knowingly mismanage their finances? The first step is changing your mindset and making the decision to get better at managing your money.

Implementing practical, effective steps and correcting behaviour deeply ingrained in us is hard; really hard. Focus and commitment are required because changing habits is all about a slow and steady process. It's a marathon, not a sprint.

In fact, information is power and this is what this whole book is about – to give you a blueprint that you can easily adopt and to provide tips and ideas on how to effectively manage your money. You probably know some of these things already and have been doing them naturally, others might be new and might be game-changing. When we started this journey, we noticed that it was really the small changes that could make a huge difference. And because no one has taught us this, we've learned it by being interested and actively doing our own research. Everything we've learned is on the pages you're reading right now.

Everyone can do this. Everyone can get better at managing their finances. It requires dedication and commitment. Much like when it comes to making healthy lifestyle choices, we need to adopt healthy spending, saving and investment habits which ultimately translate into financial well-being. To effectively manage your personal finances, taking steps to prioritise your monthly commitments and allocating funds toward savings, investments, or goals to build passive income should be a must.

A good mantra to practice is to reduce calories (debt) and build muscle (savings and investments). It's not always possible but it's what you should be aiming for. We also have debt, but we've found a way to manage it without sacrificing other areas of our lives. Individual financial situations are never black and white. But that's why having some basic money management knowledge is key – it allows you to pivot and make your money strategy your own. Some decisions that we've made might not be right for you, or how we tackle certain financial management situations might not apply to you 100%, but they might up to 80% and the rest you adjust by having the right information and knowledge on how to do so.

We don't live frugally. You certainly can if that's what you want. We live comfortably not limiting ourselves too much, but we're also mindful of where our money is going and why. We feel in control and that's what we want for you too.

So, if you are committed to the process for the long term and prepared to learn sustainable ways to manage your finances healthily, then let's get into the practical side of things.

In summary:

- Most people don't manage their money well.

- There are various financial situations you can get yourself into that lead to stress and difficulties, either short-term or long-term.

- Deciding that you want to get better control of your personal finances is the first step toward money mastering.

- Analysing how you manage your money now and where you might be doing it badly is the key thing you can do right away after reading this chapter.

# CHAPTER 3
# BLUEPRINT FOR EFFECTIVE MONEY MANAGEMENT

If 70% of us fail to manage our money well, it's not just because of bad habits or poor choices – it's also because of the lack of a consistent system for money management.

As with any commercial business, you also have a business to run dictated by your needs and money to cover for them – your life. The business of life needs proper organisation to run well too. When companies lack simple processes, issues begin. It's the same with you and your personal finances as we've discussed in the previous chapter.

So how can you be effective, efficient, and well organised with your money? This is the topic of this chapter.

**The What**

If we're truly honest with ourselves, most of us lack discipline when it comes to managing money well. Even now, we fail at it sometimes. Before, we regularly failed at being disciplined, even though Fhram is in the military and Iliyana holds a German education. No one teaches you money discipline.

Mastering money is a journey that needs a simple process you use all the time – a process that becomes ingrained in your day-to-day. This is what we call a blueprint for effective money management.

Being in control of your personal finances is a marathon, not a sprint. It's important to approach money management as a learning process. It doesn't happen overnight. We are still learning and improving too. It's the same when you go on a diet – if you attempt to lose weight with an intense, crash diet, you're bound to fail. This is because it only offers a short-term solution that does not build up good habits to ensure long-term success. The only sustainable way to achieve success in losing weight is to make certain changes such as nutritious eating, regular exercise etc. permanent. The same concept applies to money. You are in this for the long run and this book breaks things down into manageable chunks to help you change your lifestyle when it comes to your personal finances.

All you need to do is to put a plan in place that is achievable, realistic and sustainable. Taking it one day at a time is key to staying on track as expecting immediate results will only leave you disappointed which will then send you back to the unmanageable financial pit you so desperately want to exit. Putting in place small, realistic, easy-to-achieve financial changes will assist you on your path to achieving financial freedom, independence, or simply better financial control.

## The Why

A good approach to money management allows you to be well organised and helps you make good decisions. Especially if you have a partner, you need to be very clear on how you're both managing your joint money. Without an approach that's consistent daily, monthly, etc. you end up reinventing the wheel every time which is not effective and leads to poor decisions. In fact, with a good system, it's the system making many of the good decisions for you. Everything is simpler and much faster. This is what leads to efficiency.

Putting your learnings into action daily helps you build better habits so you can start becoming accustomed to this new financially healthy way of life. Once you do that, specifically on days when it feels particularly challenging, you will need to remind yourself of how you are working towards relieving financial stress in your life. Sometimes, you need to remain focused and make sacrifices for your long-term financial gain instead of deciding to act now and deal with it tomorrow. The long-term advantages of slimming down bad spending far outweigh the short-term disadvantages. It's human nature to see cutting something out of your lifestyle as a negative. The feeling of deprivation sets in because we don't look at the big picture and see ourselves five years from the day we started. Imagine what our finances would look like by then? If we change our perspective on something, we change our mindset, and the principles of money mastering are meant to improve our financial futures instead of sink us deeper into a debt pit.

Of course, when you are in financial distress, it's often difficult to focus on anything else. You get obsessed with the need to fix the issue. Anxiety consumes you; your heart rate gets elevated; you have difficulty sleeping and so on. This is why it's so important to have a reliable system to fall back on and help you get out of this.

Most importantly, a consistent approach to managing money is how you can achieve what you want. Every company has business goals and to achieve them, it also has a plan. We're talking about the same thing here. An effective system to money management is the plan and the actions you take to achieve your life goals. It's both strategic and tactical.

## The How

What is our blueprint for effective money management? It's about three key things:

1. Define your short-term, mid-term and long-term objectives.
2. Allocate the budget to cover them based on priorities.
3. Automate everything, incl. savings and investments.

Let's dive into each of these.

## Define your short-term, mid-term and long-term objectives

Mastering money starts with knowing what you want to achieve and how you make money an enabler to get there. It's all about defining your goals and creating a plan to reach them.

We look at objectives in three buckets based on the time to achieve them:

- Short-term – next few months up to a year
- Mid-term – next one to five years
- Long-terms – five years plus

Once you have your objectives defined, then it becomes much more doable to decide what steps you need to take to achieve them which includes how much money you need to allocate to each of them and with what frequency. Our brains are very powerful but often get overwhelmed by a task that at first seems difficult. This is especially true when it concerns a big sum of money at once. What our brains will accept much more easily is if that big sum of money is broken down into doable chunks on a regular basis. It's much easier for you and your bank account to pay €50 every month for six months than it is to say bye to €300 at once.

Let us explain how we approached this and give you some examples of how we've set up some of our objectives and what plans we've put in place to get achieve them.

First, we sat down and spoke about what really matters to us and how we want to live. We have done this many times and as life progresses, your priorities change. As new parents now, our number one priority is our daughter so ensuring she's covered every day is our most important task. We are also very much in agreement that we want to enjoy life and ensure we have the means to see our families every year. We're both expats so for our daughter to be able to spend time with her family members across Europe and Latin America, we need to plan for this because regular international trips can be costly, especially to a different continent. We also want to have time for ourselves as a family, so we need to plan for other vacations and experiences to build memories. Finally, we want to retire early (10 years earlier) and live in somewhere on the beach.

Being on the same page and knowing what our key priorities in life are allows us to set up specific, joint objectives which we also revisit regularly especially as we hit the short-term ones.

Here are some hypothetical examples to get you thinking:

- Short-term (next few months):
    - You may want to tackle some debt here that's particularly troubling for you and speed it up. Or this could be a short vacation you want to make.
- Mid-term (next 1-5 years):

- This can be getting ready for your wedding if you want to have a big celebration. Weddings are costly so it's one of those big things in life you may want to plan and save for in advance.
- Long-term (5+ years):
    - In this category, you could have your bigger investments such as buying property – whether to live in or to rent out.

Piece of advice here: be mindful when you're setting up your goals, especially your short-term ones. We've mentioned how the advertising world has us believe we need certain things when we don't. Take the time to deeply think about what is it that you need (perhaps it's not the new fancy car at all) and what is it that you want (perhaps more holidays abroad). Weigh these things carefully. Go deep to figure out what are your objectives – what are the things that truly matter and deserve you spending money and time on. Most of our goals are about experiences because to us, it's the memories we make that matter the most, not the stuff we buy.

What you also need to add to your planning are specific commitments or payments that always come up. These are often called sinking funds which is basically saving for irregular expenses. Most of these are either short or mid-term, at least we don't have anything long-term yet. Here are some examples:

- Short-term:
    - Christmas presents – this is not a surprising expense; it happens every year and so we prefer to not be stressed out by spending one big amount. Instead, we automatically put some money aside every month, so

we have a specific sum already gathered for when the time comes.

- o Shopping sprees – we all want to look good so from time to time renovating your wardrobe is necessary, but it can be a heavy hit on your budget. Having some already saved up funds to cover for new clothes, especially when it comes to spontaneous purchases can be of huge help and relieve you from any guilt feelings.

- Mid-term:
  - o Taxes – one thing nobody tells you when you move to the Netherlands is how much tax you pay for so many different things. Every year, we get an invoice for an incredible amount of taxes we have to pay for owning a house, for maintenance of the sewage system on the street, for garbage collection etc. We've lived in multiple other countries before and we've never seen this. So, this is not like a regular monthly expense, it's a one-off, big sum that you get in a letter via post. The first time we received it, it was a bit shocking. Now we're prepared every time as we have the money set aside.

Once you have defined what your objectives and bigger spending commitments (in addition to monthly bills) are, it's time to start looking at your budget and how and when you can allocate proportionately.

## Allocate the budget to cover your objectives based on priorities

Hopefully, you've defined goals that are realistic based on your income. You can always play around with time to achieve goals if you're a bit short on money etc. That's why starting with what you want, and then looking at what you own to figure out what you need is such an important exercise. You can always somehow make it work without putting too much pressure on yourself and staying motivated. Setting unrealistic goals, though, would have the exact opposite effect.

When you have your objectives clear, you'll have to make some decisions. Perhaps, some choices won't be that popular in the short term like cutting down unnecessary spending so that the money can go into your investments. You will need to ask yourself honest questions about where your money is going now and is it worth going there or is something else more important. The next chapter will focus exclusively on budget creation and management. We will talk about three buckets for your monthly budget:

- Basic necessities such as housing/mortgage, monthly bills, groceries etc. – 50% of your income goes here.

- Future – 30% of your income goes for savings and investments, including building up your emergency fund when you start out (more on that in Chapter 5).

- Fun such as going out with friends, shopping etc. – 20% of your income goes here and we have this on purpose because you can't live without fun. We've said it before, we're firm believers that there needs to be a balance and if you're constantly limiting yourself, you'll just explode one day in a way you probably don't want to.

When we discuss your budget in the next chapter, we will talk about journaling your spending as well. This will be a really important step. It will allow you to know where your money is currently going. Perhaps you're overspending on the fun side of things and have nothing in future you. Perhaps you have too many bills to pay – then you will need a plan to reduce that regular debt.

What's also important to understand is how to set the right priorities based on your current financial situation. A good rule of thumb when it comes to money management is to prioritise:

1. Building an emergency fund.
2. Tackling high-interest debt – anything with an interest of 7% or above (often credit cards).
3. Starting to save and invest for other priorities.

What this means is that when you start the money mastering journey, you need to first focus on getting your emergency fund (more on that in Chapter 5) and tackling high-interest debt and once you get rid of this debt, then focus on longer term investments and savings. Why do we say this? Because 7% or more of interest is a lot – you're basically losing money. The typical stock market investment gives you an annual return of 7%. So doing some basic math, if you're tackling debt and investing at the same time, you come out with 0 in the end.

It's hard to start thinking strategically about money if you haven't done so in the past. Changing your money spending and allocation habits can be challenging. And if you're someone who likes to treat yourself with new clothes, for example, we're not here to tell you to stop doing. We want to help you build a system where you're covering your monthly bills, you tackle your debt, you save and invest, and you also have room for fun. These budget categories are just guidance and something to strive for.

Not every month is going to be the same. Life happens but sticking to your objectives and your plan is what will allow you to control your money in the best way for you.

## Automate all payments, incl. savings and investments

To make it all work easily and to avoid too many temptations, you need to leverage technology and tools. Automation is your best friend in making good decisions regularly without even thinking about it.

This step is probably the simplest one in this whole chapter. It's so simple that many just don't think about it.

There's a popular saying in other books about personal finance – pay yourself first. What it means is that on the day you get your salary, you create an automatic payment coming out of your bank account and going into a savings or an investments account before you start spending for anything else. This way, you don't even see the money, so you don't have the chance to spend them on something else. The same applies to repaying debt not just savings and investments. Automation works well because as human beings, even if we say to ourselves that this month, we will save whatever is left, nothing is ever left. We spend to the last euro, it's just natural.

We've opened different savings accounts, not just one so that we can split the money based on our objectives. This way, it's not just one account with a sum of money that we then try to figure out how to allocate. It's already allocated for us. For example, you can have one savings account for a long-term objective such as buying property, you can have another savings account to gather money for a big wedding, another for big yearly commitments that you don't touch until it's time to pay for them (sinking funds), and another one for shorter-term expenses like trips or things you want to buy to allocate to when you have something left. For our savings accounts based on our goals and needs, we have set up automatic payments for every month with the amount of money we've defined, and technology does all the work for us, we don't even think about it. If debt is your main financial issues, you can do the same and automate the allocated funds to repaying it.

We also have a savings account together with our current accounts in the same bank where we separate our monthly expenses so when we get paid, we put what we will have to pay in terms of bills every month there. By doing this, we're never in a situation where we don't have money left to cover our regular bills. And because it's all in the same app, we can move it from savings to current account easily. This also allows us to plan and allocate better whatever is left after our monthly commitments.

To talk about specifically how we define the amounts, let's take a simple example of how we would do it for a last-minute trip. In this situation, we'd think about how much we need in total, look at how many months we have left until the moment we want to travel and then divide the total amount of money needed by the months left. Say we need €500 and we want to make the trip in the next five months, then we'd set up an automatic payment of €50 from Fhram's and €50 from Iliyana's current accounts to go out to our savings account for travel every month until the month we travel. This way, we almost don't feel the amount going out. The same can be applied to tackling debt, for things you want to buy for your house or any type of home improvement and even for clothes (really, for anything) – for example, if you know you will need to have a summer refresh, then you can plan for it. For anything mid-term and long-term, we would do the same: plan for it backward or if we get larger earnings throughout the year (like a bonus), we would separate them for these bigger expenses.

These tips and tricks allow you to save time and especially not delve into whether you should do something or not because it's already pre-decided for you. But you will always have to do some decision-making about personal finances which is why regular reviews of your money are important. In the next chapter, we'll dive into the details of budget management to enable the functioning of your money mastering system.

In summary, to get started with your blueprint for effective money management, you need to:

- Define your short, mid, and long-term objectives – look at what you want to achieve in the next few months, next few years and next five years and beyond.

- Analyse what you need to achieve your goals – think about what your current financial situation is like, where you're struggling and what you want to do better or change moving forward to reach the objectives you have now defined.

- Create a plan to prioritise your monthly commitments, then emergency fund and debt, then savings and investments to grow your resources. The next chapter will help you here.

- Open the required savings accounts based on your goals so you have the appropriate accounts to allocate funds as you get better at money mastering.

- Get in the habit of automating everything – create automatic bank transfers for all regular expenses as well as savings or dept repayment accounts ideally as soon as you get your salary or monthly income. You can start really small with this. It's all about practice.

# CHAPTER 4
# CREATING AND MANAGING A BUDGET

To run a successful business, companies go through a lot of planning to define their budget and how to spend it. Financial and strategy managers get assigned to this exercise. In the business of life, you are your own financial and strategy advisor (unless you hire professional help). Just as when running a business, in life, you also need to take budget planning and budget management seriously and make the time for it. In this chapter, we will talk about why this matters and how to go about it.

**The What**

Being in control of your money allows you to make the best use of it. It requires some sacrifice and discipline because it won't be handed on a golden platter. Only you can decide if you want to make the required lifestyle changes to get there. In fact, one of the most helpful changes you could make, is creating and managing a realistic budget.

A budget is an estimation of money coming and money going out during a specific period. When we talk about budgeting for personal finances, we usually focus on one month as the typical period. A budget helps you manage your monthly expenses, prepare for emergencies, focus on your future and big events in your life without going into debt. Budget management doesn't require you to be good at math. It also doesn't mean you can't buy what you want or is about spending as little money as possible feeling guilty about every purchase – this is why we're building fun into it. Finally, we don't want budgeting to be a burden for you. It's not that difficult to manage and it's simply a matter of getting in the habit of it so you know where your money is going.

You can also budget for a longer period than just a month. This is similar to the examples we've discussed in the previous chapter around working backwards from a goal by calculating how much you would need in total to achieve and the time you have.

Some might say, but how do you work off a budget when there is none? If you earn a salary, then that's your budget. Living by your means is what you will need to focus on as you start your journey to money mastering. In essence, budgeting is about having a sensible, tangible plan on how to work with the amount of money you have as opposed to "winging it" and hoping for the best. Savings, investments and tackling debt are essential parts of your budget as well, even if you are debt-free now or become debt-free one day.

Achieving financial freedom, independence or better money control may seem like an insurmountable task, but that is because when you are in a place of being financially constrained, desperation to get out of it blurs your view. The idea is to look at the easiest, least restrictive ways of creating a better management system for your personal finances. Taking it one step at a time by implementing small changes every day is how you make it work. This is why looking at budgeting is our first practical step to mastering money.

## The Why

The most important aspect of controlling your finances with a disciplined budget is consistently making month end. Without a budget, your finances will become messy leaving you with the problem of incurring further debt which can be detrimental. Your budget should be planned according to how much you earn and need to spend each month. This will give you a strategic idea of how to allocate your money for expenses and personal enjoyment based on financial limitations. Furthermore, a budget is not designed to restrict you from enjoying life but rather to ensure that you manage your finances effectively and enjoy its perks. Keeping to a fixed monthly budget will also help you stay focused on important short- and long-term goals. It will keep you more aware of what is going on with your money each month and assist you with organising and properly allocating funds to cover monthly costs.

Finances can become complicated when you have to commit to issuing the bulk of your money toward fixed monthly expenses or debt. It can become even trickier if your monthly expenses exceed your monthly income. Therefore, it is extremely important to ensure that you are not punishing yourself by overspending on your expenses per month and placing yourself in complicated and stressful financial situations. This will make controlling your finances much more difficult. We all look forward to money left over after meeting financial commitments at the end of each month. However, taking a close look at what our expenses are and knowing which expenses are fixed and which ones are redundant is important to reassess what's really needed. Looking at the ones that can be removed or reduced to relieve you of some of the pressure is also vital. Having a gym membership which you don't use regularly or at all should be cancelled as you're paying for something you're not using. It's money wasted but often we just leave it be. Reassessing your expenses will afford you additional finances that you can allocate to a savings account or do with as you wish. By agreeing to follow a budget, you force yourself to ask these questions and make good decisions or trade-offs if necessary.

Budgeting also enables you to save for unexpected emergencies and helps you tackle debt better by identifying where you can eliminate unnecessary expenditure. It also helps you plan for the big purchases and events in your life such as a house, a car, a wedding etc. This will allow you to maximise your savings or investments each month as you have a strategy in place for the things you want and the things you will need even if they're not immediate. Thinking about this and putting specific action now will give you piece of mind so that when one day you need the money to cover for these big expenses or emergencies, you already have it.

Sound financial management with a budget is important for couples as well. One of the biggest downfalls of married or cohabiting couples is a lack of communication when it comes to money. This alone leads to many avoidable problems if there was a conversation in the first place. Discussing all aspects of spending is vital to not only live a happy life together but to reduce any future conflict when it comes to money. Agreeing on what your budget should look like and how you manage it can make you both more aware of what's happening but also allow you to generate different ideas as you are planning and discussing. We often bounce off ideas when we talk about money and spending which always results in much better decisions. For us, not working with a budget is the same as spending our money without a plan. We are very clear on our goals as a family as we've discussed previously and a budget that covers our expenses, allows room for fun and enables us to save and invest for the future is helping us get to those goals with a clear path.

## The How

A good rule of thumb when it comes to creating and managing a budget is the 50-30-20 rule:

- **50% of your money goes for basic necessities** – this includes all regular expenses such as rent, mortgage, utility bills, insurance, groceries etc. Some of these are fixed (like rent and bills), others are variable (like groceries) but remain in a similar range.

- **30% of your money goes for the future** – this is where you think about savings and investments to hit your mid to long-term objectives and you build up an emergency fun (which we will discuss in the next chapter).

- **20% of your money goes for fun** – this includes going out for a drink with friends, buying new clothes etc. This is important because you need to enjoy life and enjoying life happens now.

The 50-30-20 formula is an easy rule you can follow to manage your regular salary or income. The basic idea is that you allocate all the money that comes in on a regular basis into one of the buckets so it's all allocated and you don't end up overspending. Is this super easy? No. It requires consistency and practice. We don't get it exactly as per each category every month. Life happens. Sometimes there are priorities that you can't fit in properly and you go above for whatever important reasons. But that's why you make the choice and figure out the trade-off. For example, if you have a lot of debt and you can't fit it into your 50% category, then you might want to sacrifice most of your fun category just for that, but this is a necessary step for a certain period to relieve you of the stress around debt. Maybe this month or year it will be more difficult, but the next one will be better because of the plan you're creating now. Don't forget that we don't want to make you a slave of your money. On the contrary, we want you to own your money and make sound decisions but also be flexible when it's needed.

To be able to put your money into the budget you want, you need to understand where your money goes now and whether you are spending proportionately with these categories. To achieve this, you need to start journaling and analysing your spending. Most of the time, we don't even notice where our money goes, so spending a few months tracking your expenses can be powerful. Often, it allows you to spot areas where you are spending unnecessarily or where you can cut so that you can put more into your 30% future bucket or tackle debt. This can easily be done if your regular bills and expenses are less than 50% of your monthly income. We say 50% because that's a good rule of thumb for families. More people typically will have more joint up expenses. But if you're single, your monthly financial commitments might be less than 50% giving you room to allocate more to the other buckets.

The fun category allows you to spend on random stuff because we know it always happens. There's always something special in the moment that you want or something spontaneous not planned for. And that's fine. We do it all the time but without exaggerating as we have the bucket for it that we stick to. However, be careful what you put in fun and what you put in basic necessities. A monthly payment for a luxury car is not a necessity, it's fun.

You also need to be careful because spending is like a balloon – the more money you have, the more you spend. Many people make the mistake of going through the month and deciding that whatever is left is what they'll invest or save. This never happens because as soon as you have money available to spend in your bank account, you'll spend it. The only way to be clever about this is to allocate the amount you want to invest and save and automatically transfer it out of your bank account as soon as you get your salary. As Warren Buffet – one of the richest people in the world and one of the most famous investors of all times – said: *"You don't save what's left after spending. You spend what's left after saving."* When you start budgeting like this, first plan for your 30% future bucket to build your emergency fund if you don't have one already (more on that in the next chapter) before you start investing. Always prioritise emergency fund alongside high debt, then savings and investments. And whenever you get a raise, try not to look at it as a way to spend more, rather keep your current lifestyle and allocate more to savings and investments to be able to enjoy bigger goals than just last-minute, now desires.

You need to build the discipline to use these budget categories regularly. If you end up overspending in your needs bucket for example, then you should probably sacrifice your fun bucket rather than your future bucket. Otherwise, you'll create a bad habit and every month you'll diminish the importance of saving and investment.

At the same time, remember that life happens. Not every month is the same so don't punish yourself that you haven't stuck to the buckets 100% correctly for three months in a row. Ideally, you should stick to the amounts for each of your categories but don't become a slave to them by counting to the last cent. The buckets are there to guide you, but you can't be rigid with yourself as this will just stress you out even more and make you feel guilty for not being able to do it. If it happens that you overspend in an area, then you might need to be a bit more frugal until you get your next paycheck and eat simpler dishes at home, cancelling a dinner out for example. That's all. No one died.

## CREATING AND MANAGING A BUDGET

Perhaps you can find a system to avoid unconscious overspending as well. We unsubscribe from all marketing emails; we don't have TV as in traditional TV with all ads etc. we watch Netflix so we can choose what we want to watch when we want to. Yes, we pay the subscription every month, but if we compare those €8 to what we would spend if our brains were filled with desires from advertisements, we'd be spending much more. Which is the bad thing about social media sites such as Facebook and Instagram because unless you leave the platforms, you're swamped with ideas for what more to buy. In the end, everything is about choice and the power of your mind, but if you find some tricks on how to avoid unnecessary desires, you will be better at budget management.

Let's look at some specific budget definition and management activities to start with.

**Journaling spending**

To define your budget, you need to know how much you are earning and how much you are spending over the course of a month. This is where journaling comes into play. Tracking is extremely important, especially when you don't know where your money is going. And often, you might think you know where it's going, but when you put it down on paper, you will most likely get a few surprises. Things add up and that's why it's key to know in what type of categories you spend the most as some of these might be more extreme than what you think. It could be eye-opening.

Often when you set goals and challenges for yourself in any area of your life, the only way to ensure you stick to those goals is to hold yourself accountable. Keeping a diary of your spending habits is the simplest way of doing this. It might be difficult initially, but over time you get used to it.

The beauty of keeping a spending diary is that you will be able to see where you are overspending or spending unnecessarily at a glance. This will give you the opportunity to immediately remedy any spending behaviour that doesn't speak to achieving your goals. Journaling will also reveal your wins and losses as you will be able to see where you have saved or wasted money simply by tracking how you are using the resources available to you. This will also prove as motivation to keep you on track in your journey. Notice the trends in your spending habits and make changes and adjustments as and where necessary. Remember, this is not a punishment but a strategy that will help you on your journey to effectively manage your personal finances. Journaling is the most effective way to ensure you are on track with sticking to the budget you decided for yourself.

So how do you start tracking? Here's our advice: for the next three months, write down all of your income (salary, sale of stuff, investments, any money that you receive) and all of your expenses (everything you spend money on through cards or cash). The best way to do this is to define categories where you put the specific amounts. The typical categories would be (and you could go much more detailed than that if you want):

- Income (money in):
    - Salary
    - Investment gains (if you sell shares or property income)
    - Any government help (e.g. child support)
- Expenses (money out):

- Rent/mortgage
- Groceries (all food)
- Regular bills (electricity, heating, internet, phones, insurances, subscriptions etc.)
- Debt (loans, credit card payments)
- Getting around (monthly instalments for car, petrol, tax, insurance, public transport)
- Health and medicines (doctors, dentists, prescriptions)
- Personal care (hairdressers, products etc.)
- Clothing
- Eating/drinking out (incl. takeout)
- Entertainment and hobbies (gym, classes, theatre, clubs, cinemas, concerts etc.)
- Holidays and travel
- Professional services (taxes, bank fees, legal, accounting etc.)
- Future you (savings and investments)
- One-offs (yearly payments e.g. for homeowner taxes, Christmas gifts etc.)

Categorise income and expenses from the moment you get your salary – this is when the month starts for you, regardless of whether it's the 1st or the 20th of the month. This might be confusing but after a while, you get used to it and it becomes a habit. You can opt for tracking your income and expenses with a money management app or with an excel sheet to keep track of your transactions. We use excel and we've put some easy formulas to automatically calculate what's left (income minus expenses) and hopefully, we don't get to minus with more expenses than income. You can do this daily or at the end of the week. When you start, we recommend you do this daily because at the end of the week you may not remember what certain transactions were for so daily is best for the most accurate, initial tracking to get the best view for yourself. Make sure you allocate enough time to do this because yes, it is time-consuming at the beginning but it's totally worth it.

What's important to note here is that having only one current account is key to having good visibility of what's happening with your money. If you're spending from different sources, it's difficult to track and it's also easier to spend from.

Once you get a clear view of your spending, you may find that there are a lot of adjustments that need to be made to your budget for expenses that you hadn't initially considered. Don't beat yourself up about it but rather factor those into your budget for the following month and adjust your spending accordingly. Remember, you're learning a new lifestyle and the aim is not to perfect the process overnight. The aim is to change your spending habits for the long term, one step at a time. This is a learning curve, so allow yourself to learn as you progress.

Look at your journal daily. Take the time to determine how you can begin taking steps to reduce your overspending or bad spending. Don't wait for Monday or tomorrow or the beginning of the month, start today. Spending discipline and the footprints of channelling your monthly funds will show you the points that need to be adjusted as you go along. The sooner you start, the sooner you will see results and feel the relief of regaining control of your financial well-being.

The essential elements in your budget always come first which include your fixed expenses or payments that cannot be reduced or eliminated from your budget. Remember that you need to tackle high-interest debt first before any savings or investments. Slim down on unnecessary spending in the same way that someone would cut out the calories in a healthy eating plan. There are so many little things you can do to reduce unnecessary spending and allocate that money to debt or other important areas you have decided to prioritise based on your goals. Reduce the number of times you opt to spend money on fast foods, retail stores, and other items that you feel are nice. These are not must-haves when you are on a journey to fix your finances as it will take your spending plan off budget. They are luxuries that you can live without while you are learning how to manage your finances, so cutting the number of times you buy them in a month is going to be a win for you.

Now that you've listed your fixed monthly expenses and essential items, it is time to list your needs such as fuel or transport, utilities, levies, school fees if applicable and food. There is very little flexibility in the amounts that need to be paid for these items monthly other than food. Grocery lists are the first place that you can start to slim down on spending as it is easily achieved by working on a budget. Cooking rather than eating out is by far the best option for your health and your pocket.

Utilities are also flexible to a degree and can be reduced if you make yourself aware of your consumption. You could use the shower as opposed to the bath. Remember to turn off the lights in rooms that are not used. All it takes is a conscious effort to make minor behavioural changes and then the discipline to stick to the plan of budgeting will come into play. If you're serious about achieving financial freedom, making that effort will become second nature once you have learned how to.

The next things to add to your budget are your loan and credit card repayments. Make sure that you are paying at least the minimum repayment required by the creditor. It's essential that you pay these diligently every month. We repay credit cards 100% of the amount the next month with nothing left for the future. In fact, we only have a credit card for the situations when we cannot pay by debit card, otherwise, we'd get rid of them – they're a pure temptation.

Next, review the various subscriptions and contracts that you already have in place and determine if they are necessary. This is where you can make substantial cutbacks in your finances which will allow for a healthier financial position. This includes subscriptions like Netflix, Spotify and other streaming services as well as gyms etc. Ask yourself how often you make use of them and if it is really necessary to keep all of these subscriptions. It's advisable to select your favourite ones and the ones you really use and get rid of the rest. Having too many unnecessary subscriptions that you don't use often but have to pay only adds to financial constraints. If you absolutely have to keep them all then opt for a reasonable package instead of the full bouquet. It's a small sacrifice to make and if you really investigate it, you'd see that you're paying for numerous channels that you don't even watch. By doing this, you will notice an immediate saving on your monthly bottom line and whatever you have saved can be redirected to paying off another debt.

You can also look at your mobile phone contract. Do you have the best deal in line with your affordability or are you paying an arm and a leg for the latest phone? If you use your phone for business, then the latter would be feasible, however, if you just use it for phone calls and browsing social media, then migrating to a lower package would cut costs. Nowadays, it's essential to have a mobile phone, but there is always the possibility of downgrading your plan or moving to a pay-as-you-go plan once your contract comes to an end. This should be kept in mind the next time you're due to upgrade unless having the best phone on the market to keep up with trends is your aim. In this case, if you're on a tight financial constraint, your monthly budget would take a hit.

Revisit your going out expenses as well. If you're a person who is used to socialising, consider changing the things that you do in your social life. Instead of meeting at a coffee shop every time, rather meet at a park and go for a walk with your friends. Find things to do that don't always cost money. Although this is a small sacrifice, in time you will feel the benefits of it. Having to spend money you didn't budget for, no matter how small the amount, eventually adds up and you realise it too late. Additionally, going out means spending money so reducing the number of times you go out on social dates can be beneficial when facing financial constraints. If your weekly socialising dates demand four days per week, reduce it to two where you spend and two for activities that are free.

All these are just ideas to cut expenses here and there. Individually, they might sound small but when you add up and especially when you calculate not just the monthly, but the yearly amount of saving by cutting down, it can become quite the sum. For example, treating yourself to a cappuccino of just €3 every day, adds up to €21 a week, €84 a month and €1,008 a year.

Finally, list how much you're saving and investing. Perhaps it's nothing now because you need to prioritise debt, that's okay. But over time, you'll start to be able to put money into this category as well and it's important to track how much it is so that you can eventually get to the 30%.

## Maximising what you have

Because of unhealthy spending habits and too much debt, many people find themselves in the position of more money out than money in. What you earn on a monthly basis can only go so far if you don't use the right strategies and have a budget plan in place. If you are overspending money unnecessarily and not working off a budget, then maxing out your salary before the new month begins is because of negligent spending. Ultimately, don't live a life you can't afford. Focus on maximising what you have now and spending it the best way possible without going into debt. As you reduce debt, you can start focusing on growing your money not just managing it.

Earning more money requires smart thinking and strategising. As you advance through your career, set salary and growth goals for yourself. Just like you would set yourself goals for your financials, devise a salary strategy. Set short, medium and long-term goals that are market-related to the position you hold or the job you see yourself doing in the future. Make sure that your salary goals are in cahoots with the personal financial strategies you have set for yourself. The key as we have said several times is that these goals need to be realistic and achievable. Don't put yourself up for failure or disappointment by expecting too much and be prepared for whatever outcome you eventually land on, salary-wise.

Another easy thing to consider here is selling things. Over time, we all accumulate stuff that we thought we needed but didn't. These are things that we no longer use that have now been shoved to the back of a cupboard. It's the same with clothes and shoes you no longer like or fit. The latter is especially true about children's clothes. Something that may no longer be of value to you could be a treasure to someone else, so why not get rid of all those unwanted items and generate some cash? The rewards are two-fold as you'd have a little cash in your pocket and get a spring clean you didn't plan on doing, not to mention the extra cupboard or garage space it would afford you. You can easily use Facebook Marketplace or Vinted. This is also a way to generate a bit for your fun bucket – sell something to buy something new. That way you won't feel as guilty if you're restrained financially.

Maintenance of your possessions is an essential aspect of managing your finances effectively and maximising what you have without incurring new spending as well. It's a lot more affordable to maintain your assets as opposed to neglecting them to reach the point of total disrepair. If this happens then you will have to spend a bunch to restore them to reliable working order or opt for getting yourself into more debt by replacing them. For example, even if you feel like you can't afford the cost of regular servicing of your car, making sacrifices to properly maintain it will be far less trouble than neglecting it until it breaks. If you decide to sell your car one day, a car with a full-service history has a much higher market value than one that doesn't. Small steps like this will eventually lead you to a consistent life of financial well-being.

Most importantly, maintaining your health through healthy eating and exercise will also reduce the amount of money you need to spend on medical aid. It's no secret that the cost of basic health care, whether it involves a simple visit to the doctor, or a hospital stay can be expensive. By taking care of your health, you can reduce the amount of money needed to spend on healthcare. Medical insurance is an essential expense in your monthly budget. In the same way that it's essential that you pay your rent or home loan monthly, it's of paramount importance that you have adequate funding or medical insurance in place in the event of an accident or emergency. Although it may be considered an unnecessary grudge purchase because it's one of those things that you may never need, it's essential in times that you do need it. Although taking care of your health can reduce your chances of becoming ill often, it does not negate the fact that you need a medical insurance or a hospital plan in place to accommodate such occurrences.

Mental health is another critical issue that we often neglect when it comes to financial mismanagement. Most of us may think that asking for help or admitting we're not coping is a sign of weakness. It's not, it's why you're reading this book. It was created to help those in financial distress cope with their situation by making small changes. Taking the necessary steps to ensure financial well-being directly impacts emotional well-being as well.

**Avoiding unnecessary consumerism**

The worse mistake we all make is by feeding an advertiser's dream. The purpose of effective advertising is to lure a consumer into believing that this item is something that you now absolutely have to have. Don't be the consumer that believes those mistruths. Be content with what you do have and appreciate the hard work it has taken to achieve that. You don't have to stay up-to-date with the latest trends if it's affecting your financial health. It's good to refresh your closet from time to time but is it really necessary for you to replace your entire wardrobe each time a new trend hits the market? Most likely not.

By avoiding unnecessary consumerism, you avoid debt which is strategic. If you reassess what brings you contentment in life and place less value on material possessions, you are already one step closer to avoiding unnecessary consumerism. You don't have to live your life trying to impress anyone by spending money and living by societal expectations. It's your life.

Over recent years, we've learnt a truly valuable lesson that most retired people will tell you. Most of the world spend their lives working themselves to death to buy beautiful homes and drive flashy cars. The sad thing is that they never enjoy those things that they simply had to have because they are too busy working. Although spending on the luxuries that life has to offer does have its perks if it fits your budget, according to research, a spike in the "feel good" hormone Dopamine is more evident in people who spend on memorable experiences with those they care for. This, in fact, is beneficial to mental health rather than the downward spiral caused by stress after unnecessary spending.

Of course, our lifestyles change as we move further along our career paths and with that comes greater earning potential. When this happens, you don't have to spend more because you earn more. Just because you may reach a point where you are able to upscale your lifestyle doesn't mean that you have to. If you're content with your life as it is, why change? The TV that you have had until now should not be replaced if it is still in perfect working condition. Unless there have been some drastic changes in the demographics of your life, the house you own should be enough. If the car you are driving is perfectly functioning and reliable, there is no valid reason to upgrade it for the sake of acquiring the latest model. What we're trying to say is be satisfied with what you have if it is still functional. Don't place value on possessions because there will always be something bigger and better and you will spend your life chasing a dream that will keep you in debt. It's a vicious circle that becomes your own personal brand of addiction which can have you spinning out of control. If you look at the digital age we live in where the latest trends are being upgraded at a pace that is impossible to keep up with, buying them is not necessary, especially if it's going to set you back financially.

If you really want something but don't have the full amount of money to buy it in cash, there are other options in which you could obtain it. If you look at the blooming Facebook Marketplace and other online markets, you may find the same items, whether used or brand new at a more affordable price. Maybe someone no longer has use for them and has decided to sell, so honing in all your options will be a double win for you as you'd get what you wanted at a much cheaper price.

There's one important thing we want to mention here. There are people who choose to live frugally, meaning they optimise their resources to the maximum. We do that in certain areas, in other areas we think about what's more expensive – paying for something or doing it ourselves. When you choose to do it yourself, that requires your time. And your time is money, as the famous saying goes. It's good to know how much your time is worth on an hourly basis as that can help you make certain decisions. One example where we choose to pay because it's more expensive to do it ourselves (we came up to that conclusion after making some basic calculations) is to have someone come and clean the house every two weeks. So be smart about where you put your time too, not just your money.

It's very easy to fall prey to unnecessary spending, but there are also effective ways to curb it. According to statistics, the most effective way of avoiding unnecessary spending is to work on a budget and off a list of items you need. As there is a plan and purpose for everything, the same will apply to spending. Wandering up and down the store aisles with no plan of what you should buy will result in unnecessary purchases that exceed your budget. Or falling prey to the big sings saying 40% outside of a shop is just a temptation to buy something you probably don't need just because it's on offer.

If you find shopping with a list and sticking to it an impossible task because you might just need something else here or there, then cut yourself some slack and have one cheat day that has a capped budget to satisfy your craving. Additionally, you can also opt to do online shopping whereby you avoid physically walking up and down the aisles and work off your list. There are stores that offer a delivery service, which will avoid you from putting yourself in a position to be tempted to spend money unnecessarily. Just like how someone who's trying to achieve weight loss usually steers clear from bakeries with all the delicious pastries on display in glass cabinets, you can also avoid exposing yourself to the temptation of unnecessary overspending by physically shopping in-store. The key to achieving the rhythm of money mastering is to make slow and steady realistic, achievable changes that will eventually become a lifestyle. Cut out those unnecessary financial calories and before you know it, the results will speak for themselves.

The purpose of budget management is about building healthy spending habits and having a plan to manage your personal finances effectively. What we've discussed in this chapter are all examples of things you can try. In the end, your life is yours. Everyone is different. Everyone has different needs and is in a different situation that requires different strategies. What we want you to take out from this chapter is a structured way of approaching your monthly budget management. Living well while being self-sufficient is a privilege available to all but practised by a few. Limiting your spending doesn't mean that you should tie yourself down and cut off enjoyment. You work hard so you're entitled to enjoy your money, but how are you to do so if there's none left? Finding ways to effectively manage your finances is a means to afford you the opportunity to find the best ways to spend your money, to still have the choice of enjoying life while saving, to invest in your future, and to take care of debt with precision.

When it comes to money mastering, the aim is not to be overly restrictive and go on a crash diet as then failure is imminent. Taking it all in at once can be overwhelming and it's better to take baby steps one day at a time. Making small changes to your finances is key to achieving your goals.

In summary, here are the key actions you can take now:

- Create an excel spreadsheet or choose an app to begin journaling your income and expenses – do this very diligently for at least the first three months to gain a good understanding of your current spending.

- Schedule these budget reviews like an appointment – put them in your diary at a specific, repeating cadence. We have them recurring in Google Calendar. Look at this month but also next month and the one after to spot upcoming birthdays or big, irregular expenses etc. so you can plan for them if necessary.

- Bucket your spending in a budget that breaks spending into three categories:
    o 50% of spending goes to necessities and recurring bills.
    o 30% goes into future savings and investments (with your emergency fund being priority which we will discuss in the next chapter).

- 20% goes into fun (unless you have a ton of debt, so you should leverage this category to get rid of it as soon as possible).
- Analyse how much money goes in and how much goes out and what for – identify where are you overspending and define ways to cut on spending that's unnecessary.
- Get in the habit of challenging your thinking about what is it that you really need versus just want and decide if the desires are worth spending on. Sometimes just waiting 10 minutes and thinking about it might change your mind and you may no longer want it.
- Over time, strive to stick to the 50-30-20 rule as much as you can once you get cleared of debt and can focus on savings and investments.

# CHAPTER 5
# BUILDING AN EMERGENCY FUND

Have you ever heard of Murphy's law? It's an adage that says: *"Anything that can go wrong will go wrong."* This law applies to businesses and individuals alike as life can be unpredictable. It's also why people talk about a plan B so you can be prepared for situations when things don't go quite right. Surprises and unexpected events will always occur (think COVID), so you should be prepared for them financially as well.

We spent the previous chapters talking about how to follow an effective system and a budget to manage your money. Being armed with this knowledge, now it's time to figure out how to build your emergency fund as your first priority item to be able to address unanticipated occurrences.

**The What**

An emergency fund is a sum of money that you have easily at your disposal, but you don't use it unless it's necessary because of certain unpredictable events. The emergency fund is separate from your monthly income as well as any other types of savings and investments. Typically, the amount of this fund is the amount of money needed to cover all living expenses for three to six months. This money is stashed away in a separate bank account you can easily access but don't withdraw from because the emergency fund is just for emergencies – situations of serious financial distress that are unanticipated. Perhaps you lost your job, your car broke and you need an immediate fix as otherwise you can't get to work, you need to do major house repairs, you have a medical emergency, a funeral to attend etc. Your emergency fund is used for serious things that cost money you don't have in your pocket right now or that your insurance doesn't cover.

To give you an example, an issue with the heating of your house could easily cost you €2,000-3,000. With an emergency fund already available, you can have peace of mind that you can tackle this issue without stress. Having built up sufficient resources to get a solution to a problem will reduce the worry of getting through this unforeseen circumstance and give you ample time to organise and implement your next steps. Having a financial safety net is essential to get through the battle of an unexpected situation even in the case of loss of income. It almost sounds unrealistic to expect someone already living from salary to salary to have a financial buffer built up for situations like this. But if you teach yourself how to effectively manage your money, you will be better placed to contribute, even in the smallest way, to an emergency fund. Knowing that those resources will be readily available to you should the need arise will give you peace of mind if you are ever faced with an emergency.

And please note that a last-minute vacation is not an emergency.

## The Why

No one's job is truly safe. If you work for a corporation, being laid off due to downsizing or a takeover is always a possibility. There have been plenty of examples in the first half of 2022, especially in the tech industry (Tesla, Netflix and more). If you work for a small company, it could die due to lack of success or be bought out. Consider what happened at the beginning of 2020 during the COVID pandemic – so many people lost their income, so you should always be prepared for a job loss by having at least three months worth of living expenses in the bank because you never know what might happen. If you know the amount you're bringing in and spending each month, which is what we covered in the previous chapter, it's easier to accumulate this financial cushion.

Although this is self-explanatory to a degree, there are several reasons why having an emergency fund is essential, particularly in today's economic state. The purpose of having an emergency fund is to take care of life's unexpected events without having to incur further debt to do so. Of course, the most obvious reason would be for emergency medical expenses, but there are other reasons. You may find yourself in a position where you get ill and are forced to be on sick leave for a period that exceeds your sick leave allowance. This means that any additional days of sick leave that you take will be seen as unpaid leave unless you have accrued annual leave that you can use in lieu of unpaid leave. If you don't, however, having an emergency fund in place means that while you are not earning an income, you are still able to pay your bills and meet your financial commitments without having to worry. Further to that, most medical insurances or medical aids don't always cover all expenses in full and you can be faced with shortfall accounts that amount to thousands. Your emergency fund is there to ensure that these shortfalls are paid without having to reach for your credit card, take out another loan or max your overdraft.

Another reason for having an emergency fund available to you is for maintenance. Imagine that suddenly your car needs to undergo extensive repairs that fall outside of your vehicle's warranty. Having an emergency fund in place means that you will have access to it immediately and will be able to undertake the necessary repairs required to restore your car to reliable running order. The other side of it is that new tyres for a car can be costly and having an emergency fund available to you will help you replace them. After all, your safety depends on it.

The same principle applies if you are a homeowner. If you are faced with sudden substantial expenses for unforeseen emergency repairs to your home, having an emergency fund available to you means that the repairs can be undertaken without having to incur debt or further damage to your property. This is especially the case if you have any plumbing or heating issues which can cost you at least €2,000-3,000 to fix and if you don't have it, can you imagine yourself without water or heat in the middle of winter? While this may seem like very basic, logical advice, when you are in financial distress, these are the last things you think about.

In the event of loss of income which we have seen on prolific scales in the last couple of years, with an emergency fund in place, you will still be able to meet your monthly financial commitments without incurring further debt to do so. The same would apply to losing your job completely and still having to face the same debt at the end of the month with no income to cover your expenses. This is why we recommend building up funds to cover costs for at least three months to buffer any loss of income for the foreseeable future.

If you are a contractor or a freelancer and rely on securing projects as your source of income, it's particularly essential that you have an emergency fund in place to carry you through the months where you have no contracts or lesser contracts than normal. To not affect your ability to continue paying your bills until such time as you are able to generate a regular income again, the emergency funds that you put aside in the previous months will be your aid and carry you through. As a contractor, you are further impacted when it comes to being unable to generate an income as a result of an economic crisis as there are no funds to derive an income from and you are pretty much on your own when it comes to finding a means to compensate for this loss of income or inability to earn.

To give you an example of the gravity of how unprepared most people are, a 2020 survey by the Federal Reserve in the United States found that more than 25% of Americans lacked the ability to cover a $400 unexpected expense. Among unemployed workers, that figure rose to 45%. [iv]

Finally, if you are saving towards a financial goal like a deposit on a new house or purchasing a new car, in the event of an emergency arising, you won't have to dig into that fund and experience a setback if you have an allocated emergency fund. Since the aim of money mastering is to manage your personal finances effectively, having an emergency fund in place when life happens is so valuable. And you should start contributing to an emergency fund now, even with just a small amount at the beginning but on a regular monthly basis.

**The How**

As mentioned, a good rule of thumb for your emergency fund is to save 3-6 months of your monthly expenses. The decision whether you accumulate three or six months depends on your personal situation and on what you're comfortable with. If have a big family, you might choose six months rather than three. If you're single, three months might be enough.

The emergency fund money should go into a separate account you can easily access but forbid yourself to do so unless it's an emergency as discussed above. Always ensure that the funds are kept in a savings account that generates the highest interest possible while making sure that it will be available immediately without a waiting period when you need it. If you don't have such a bank account, do your research and open it – look for the highest interest rates and ensure the bank has a policy to cover any losses should the bank itself go bankrupt, meaning they will return your money in full if something happens to their business.

Since we've already spoken about budget and you've hopefully started journaling your spending, you should be able to easily calculate how much you would need for your emergency fund simply by multiplying your monthly commitments by three or up to six. Say you need €3,000 to cover all your bills and spending necessities in a given month, then you would need to set €9,000 aside to cover for three full months. When you know the amount needed, decide on a timeframe to achieve gathering it and work backwards to calculate how much you should be depositing to your emergency fund monthly. If your goal is to build your emergency fund within two years, then you would need to save €375 a month (€9,000 divided by 24 months).

Building an emergency fund should fall into your 30% future bucket as discussed in the previous chapter, however, we always recommend prioritising the emergency fund above anything else because you never know what might happen. If you can sacrifice parts of your 20% fun bucket by reducing these expenses (we've given you plenty of examples on how to do so in the previous chapter), you would be able to accumulate the emergency resources much faster. What this also means is that you should focus on allocating that 30% of your income purely on gathering your emergency fund before you even start saving for other things or investing. However, if you live paycheck by paycheck barely making ends meet and cannot yet divide your monthly budget to the 50-30-20 rule, then try to at least allocate 2% of your paycheck to your emergency fund. Even a small financial safety net of just a month worth of expenses can help you out when you most need it.

When you know the exact monthly amount, ensure that you have an automatic transfer on the day you get paid that sends the money into your emergency fund savings account. This way, the funds go out without you even noticing, so you would not be tempted to spend them on something else. Also, ensure you're not touching the money that has accumulated in your emergency fund account. There's no point in saving regularly when you constantly take away from the account. The account is meant for emergencies only and you need to let the money sit there until you reach the amount you have defined.

Another thing you can consider is to allocate your entire tax refund – that's money you get back from the government if you overpay on taxes in a year – to your emergency fund. So instead of spending your tax refund on various other things, you can deposit it to your emergency fund account and that way you can reach your emergency fund goal much faster.

We got into building our emergency fund a bit unexpected as we didn't know about emergency funds at the time. Each of us had started saving monthly. We were automatically depositing money each month. Over time, the amounts grew and when we got together, we saw that we had accrued our emergency fund without even noticing as it was happening automatically and we could now focus on saving and investing for the bigger events and goals in our lives.

When it comes to personal finances, it's all about priorities. The best way to have resources to draw from for unexpected expenses is to save. You may say that you don't have enough money to pay bills, so how are you expected to save. Simple, by reassessing your current expenses. Spending your money each month on things that are not necessary can become a problematic habit with time. It can stand in the way of you being in control of your finances. Buying new things can be exciting, but if you're looking to start curbing your spending and taking control of it, then it may be time to put a hold on it for a little while. And you don't have to limit yourself completely. You can make small changes for a while until you get to a point where you have peace of mind. Say you tend to eat takeaway food most of the time per week. That's a big cost and not to mention not good for your health. Cooking your food can help you save money and it's more nutritious. If you work outside of your house, why not cook and bring your lunches? You don't have to cut out all takeaway but simply reduce. For example, instead of eating out six times a week, reduce that to three times a week. Say one takeout costs €15 per person. You'd be then saving €45 a week which adds up to €180 a month and €2,160 a year. In addition, you typically spend another €60 a week to go out for drinks or social events. You decide to cut that in half, so you save €30 a week which becomes €120 a month and €1,440 a year. Now let's also say you spend €40 a month on a gym membership you don't really use so you decide to cancel it. Adding these three reductions, you now have €340 (€180+€120+€40) available to allocate to your emergency fund – almost the amount needed in the above example to save €9,000 in two years. Reassessing your spending habits can help you gain control and allow you to build your emergency fund which is a far bigger priority than short-lived enjoyments.

Evaluating what you need for the month and not what you want is key to overcoming overspending and to building a savings muscle. The experience of self-discipline when spending may be enough to change your outlook on the process. When money is limited, you would be surprised at how you manage to pull through without spending as much as you might have been used to. Now imagine the perks of doing that every month. The long-term rewards are fruitful, especially when you put an actual number to it.

And if you're the type of person that struggles with self-control, technology is here to help. Look at savings in the same way as you would an expense. Condition yourself to see savings as a bill that must be paid like all your other regular expenses and then pay it no matter the amount automatically by adding a fixed savings amount transfer to your emergency fund account. However, be careful not to put yourself under additional financial strain by depositing an amount that is heavily off-budget. You need to make the goal achievable. Saving for an emergency fund while neglecting current high-interest debt is an illogical approach. It would be more sensible to allocate funds to each commitment, so that you pay off your high-interest debt rather than have it increase and at the same time have small amounts of money gaining muscle in your emergency account. It's not a financially sound decision to have money in the bank and ignore your debt as it'll keep accumulating and you want to get rid of paying high interest. Notice how we're talking about high-interest debt here that we will cover in detail in the next chapter, but it's important to prioritise your emergency fund alongside any debt with an interest rate of 7% or above because that's a lot of money you're losing simply by loaning money from someone else.

To summarise, here's how you take action to get to your emergency fund:

- Look at your spending journal and identify how much you need every month to pay all your financial commitments and survive the month. Multiply that by at least three (up to six) and that's the amount you need for your emergency fund.

- Set yourself a goal with a clear timeline when you want to have built up your emergency fund but don't make that timeline too long. Think short to mid-term.

- Calculate backwards from that timeline and identify the amount you need to deposit monthly to ensure you can gather the whole amount by the time you've decided.

- Try to bucket this amount into your 30% future budget category every month. If it goes above, reassess your 20% fun bucket spending and sacrifice this bucket, but don't go into additional debt to pay for an emergency fund. You need a balanced monthly budget.

- Get in the mindset that saving for an emergency fund is more important than wearing the latest fashion clothes, for example.

- Be proud of yourself as your emergency fund begins to grow even if you've started with a small amount. Every little win is worth celebrating.

- Once you have saved for your entire emergency fund, don't stop saving but rather reallocate those monthly deposits to another goal (more on that in Chapter 7) and return to your usual 20% fun bucket if you've had to sacrifice it. The more you practice money mastering, the more your quality of life should increase and the less you'll have to sacrifice. Look at sacrifice as temporary and stay motivated to achieve your goals and enjoy your successes.

- If you ever use up parts of your emergency fund, put a plan in place to return to its original amount again.

BUILDING AN EMERGENCY FUND

# CHAPTER 6
# TACKLING DEBT

The most difficult thing about money mastering is learning to live with what you have and not with what you wish you had. The latter is what gets you into debt, whereas the former is what allows you to improve your quality of life as time progresses. But ever since credit cards were invented, debt has become a way of living for many, which most of the time hurts their financial situation.

While some of us have an average amount of debt, others have accumulated hefty bills from negligent spending alongside complicated financial situations. Having to pay high bills every month is frustrating but managing and reducing debt involves diligent practice, which ultimately leads to a stress-free life. In this chapter, we will talk about how you can better tackle debt.

### The What

Debt is an almost certain eventuality once we have settled into adulthood, especially once we have decided to start our own families. As much as we would like to avoid it, it's nearly impossible with the cost of living today. Debt is money you borrow from someone else, typically a banking institution, but it could be an individual as well. You need to return the money in a certain timeframe paying interest on top of the borrowed amount. It's a way to pay for something you don't have the money for right now.

The most common types of debt are loans – mortgage loans, car loans, student loans, and credit cards. The first three you normally borrow from a financial institution which scrutinises your current financial situation and ability to repay the loan before they give it to you. The interest they receive is a way to ensure they're compensated for the risk they're taking on you by lending you the money and to motivate you to repay it faster. Credit cards, on the other hand, have a rolling timeframe depending on how you set up your repayments, and the amount changes regularly as you continue to use your credit card.

Reading finance books, you will often find this classification of debt:

- **Secured debt** – involves collateral that is pledged by you in exchange for a loan. These include larger amounts which are usually home loans or vehicle finance. The home or car that you purchased serves as collateral and can be repossessed at any time if you fail to meet the payment agreement.

- **Mortgaged debt** – is a loan that is used to purchase property. This includes any type of real estate purchases. The lender attaches a substantial amount of interest to the original loan amount that the borrower agrees to pay over a period.

- **Unsecured debt** – is money lent without collateral. It includes credit card expenses, medical bills, rentals, utilities etc. The lender takes a risk in lending to the borrower who usually obtains the chance to acquire the credit because of credit scoring.

- **Revolving debt** – is money in and money out according to how the borrower sees fit. Although it comes with interest rates, paying it back will depend on how it's used. It's an account or credit option that allows borrowing irrespective of the credit line. It has no scheduled payment date or fixed amount that is payable monthly.

For us, when we look at debt, we classify it into good and bad, depending of course on your financial situation and whether you can repay it, how high the interest rate is and whether having to pay debt prevents you from saving and investing.

Good debt can help you build wealth — like a mortgage. Property is an asset that usually increases in value unless we face a financial crisis. In the Netherlands, mortgages are financed 100% without the need for a down payment which makes them very attractive. Owning a property is cheaper than renting, so many choose to buy a house or an apartment. Some buy a second one to rent it as an investment and a second income stream. That's not the case in all countries, so you need to be mindful of the conditions depending on where you live. Another example of good debt is a student loan because it's an investment in your future potential through education that can open doors to you for a better start in life and a more successful career.

Bad debt, on the other hand, brings you no return and little or no benefits over time. For many people, this type of debt has become a means to build the life that they want, ignoring the life that they need, which is more affordable. This is the case of abusing credit cards. Also, a mortgage is a debt you can't avoid, but a car that you don't have the means to afford but buy by borrowing to keep social appearances is a debt you get yourself into. The second one is especially tricky because it can become an addiction and because it's driven by societal pressures you have in your head. This is especially concerning when you end up borrowing a second loan or opening a second credit card to be able to pay for the first.

## The Why

Many people get stuck in the vicious circle of bad debt, not knowing how to get out of it. They get so bogged down with the now that they forget that by doing little by little, they can get out of debt, but they need to remain focused and make sacrifices for a certain amount of time. "I'll figure it out tomorrow" is not a good strategy for financial management. It's not a strategy at all. It's irresponsible. Rather, what is needed is a debt management plan in place to manage debt and get it under control for the long term.

Why does this matter? Simple – you would live a less stressful and more fulfilled life without the presence of bad debt that inevitably controls you. Avoiding accumulating debt allows you to better control your finances along with becoming financially independent. Paying off your debt quickly gives you the chance of changing your financial circumstances and gaining financial satiety.

One of the biggest debt issues is credit card debt which comes with a heap of temptation to spend. People in the United States have an absolute mountain of credit card debt in 2022 - $841 billion in total![v] The average credit card balance in 2021 for Americans was $5,525[vi]. It's easy to be tempted to use your credit card when you are short on cash, and you really want to buy something you don't really need. Even during those months where you fall short of cash and need your credit card to get you through, then again, the spending frenzy starts without calculating the consequences. So, what happens in the months that follow, after you have spent on your credit card? Your repayments increase and so does your interest rate. It's a vicious cycle that doesn't stop spinning and if you ever calculate how much interest rate you pay, you would be shocked. Many don't pay attention to the amount of interest you have to pay because getting a credit card is so simple that you don't look at the paperwork at all. In fact, credit card debt can cost you 10% to 30% in interest per year[vii].

Most debt occurs because of overspending. As we've discussed in the previous chapters, the majority of us don't sit to identify what those reasons are and apply strategies to curb them. Often people overspend because of their desire to impress others. It's very easy to fall into the trap of comparing ourselves to others and wanting to live their lives. If we are completely honest with ourselves, we have to admit that in one way or another, we all do it in various areas of our lives. If you take appearance as an example, we often look at celebrities and compare ourselves to them. We sometimes aspire to have their bodies, beauty, and glamourous lifestyles. The reality is that they don't even have that perceived perfection themselves. If we removed all the make-up, hair brushing, and hours in front of a stylist, we'd change our perspective. So why do we aspire to be copycats of a camouflage? It's because we spend too much time comparing ourselves to others.

The same can be said for our financial positions. Overspending as a result of trying to impress others is a dangerous game to play, particularly when we don't have a clear picture of what that person's financial status is. They could also be living in debt on a quest to impress others, so comparing ourselves to them is not a healthy way of living and will eventually only drag us into further debt because we want to keep up. A good quote to keep in mind here is what world's seventh wealthiest person Warren Buffett once said: *"If you buy things you do not need, soon you will have to sell things you need."*

If you find that your overspending is directly related to meeting a deeper-seated need that is born from obligation, then meeting that need as best you can is the best option. However, making that need a habit will have detrimental results as you would sink yourself deeper into the pits of debt. The only time resulting symptoms will automatically begin to remedy themselves is if you don't give in to temptation and remain focused. If you keep asking yourself the "why" questions and then answer them honestly, you will fall into temptation less often. It all depends on whether or not you're honest about the reason behind your overspending habits.

Another reason people tend to overspend is that in this day and age, we live in a world of instant gratification. When we want something, it has to be now or never. Most of us don't want to waste time saving for it, so we take out loans to buy it immediately without considering the months that wait ahead when we'd have to dish out the payments whether we like it or not. One of the key factors of money mastering is patience as that is the cue to eventually achieve financial independence. Having the patience to save the money you need to buy that specific item will avoid a monthly instalment that has added interest rates leading you to pay double or triple the loan you hastily took out.

The time it takes you to save the money to buy the items you wanted may be a blessing in disguise. You might realise that you no longer need them by this time and could let the savings accumulate without even realising or use them to pay off another existing debt. Seeing that it could possibly be a lump sum by then, you could redirect those funds any way you think would be beneficial to your financial future rather than abiding by your immediate temptation that once you get it, you most likely will forget about soon as it only brings you a short amount of happiness.

The reality is that most people are not pragmatic about debt. They just get used to it and are afraid of changing their current lifestyle to tackle it. Easy money and immediate gratification are stronger than future planning. Imagine you've been in deep debt over the past five years, paying off a great car that you're not really enjoying because you're stressing about the monthly amount you have to pay and where you will get it from. In addition, you buy these beautiful clothes that you're also not enjoying because you've paid for them with your credit card that you don't know how you will cover next month. Wouldn't it be better to sacrifice some of those items that you're not in the position of having now for next two years, get your life together, put a budget in place, start saving and investing and then become able to afford these things as well as truly enjoy them? That's the type of life you should be striving for because then you can truly celebrate your achievements and be proud of the hard work you've put in.

**The How**

As you're reading this, how much money have you borrowed that you need to pay this month? If you don't know it at the top of your head and can't tell immediately, then you're not managing your debt very well or you're not managing it at all.

If you've followed the steps from Chapter 4, you should have an idea of your fixed monthly expenses, including debt. You need to make sure you take a sharp look at it and break it down into what each of your debt items is for, how much they cost you monthly, how much interest you pay and what the timeframe is to repay them. Having all your debt in front of you will allow you to see the bigger picture and perhaps surprise you a bit as you may not have realised how much it was in total. Try to compile three lists:

1. Good debt that can bring you a return (property loans or student loans etc.).
2. Bad debt that brings you no return (debt that you're paying because you're living above your means, including credit cards).

Now look at how you can prioritise each debt item within each list based on the highest interest rate or its importance – from the most difficult at the top to the easiest to tackle at the bottom. Anything that's 7% interest and above becomes your priority alongside your emergency fund. Or if there's another debt that is stressing you out more, then this becomes the most important one. You need to get rid of this top debt as soon as possible because you're losing money by paying so much interest or you're spending sleepless nights worrying about it. Here's where creating a plan comes into play, especially reducing spending in other areas to be able to cover the outstanding debt that you need to prioritise.

Once you have your list and have determined what the minimal amount is for each debt item, look at your fixed monthly expenses and look at the remaining income you have to establish how much more you can put aside toward these debts to pay them off quicker. Taking a long time to pay off debt isn't going to serve you in any way as it will only hamper opportunities that come your way. If you stick to your plan, as you progress one day at a time you will notice how you'll be freeing yourself from stress and money wasting into money allocated to savings, investments, holidays and much more. The goal is to eliminate debt to enjoy a life of freedom and less worry.

Focusing on getting rid of one debt fast doesn't mean ignoring the rest of your debt and fixed monthly commitments. Your budget plan needs to ensure you have what you need to cover for at least the minimum repayment required as part of your 50% necessities bucket because if you miss one, you will accumulate more interest to pay, setting you back. Use tools to help you by automating all these payments and if it's not possible, put calendar reminders so you don't forget and pay on time. And most importantly, ensure all this debt is listed in your budget regardless of whether you use an app or an excel sheet. Keeping track of debt and your debt repayments monthly is key to having visibility on how you're doing and ensuring you're not missing a payment. It can also show you progress over time, especially if you have to sacrifice some or most of your 20% fun bucket from your budget to cover debt. By journaling, you will be able to spot how your 20% fun bucket returns to normal once you've repaid debt and this is a great achievement if debt was a big issue for you.

If you're in an extreme debt situation where you can barely afford to put food on the table because of so much debt and future planning or resources for fun are completely out of the question, then you may need an extreme solution. You should still list all your debt and rank it based on importance and you may have to make some difficult decisions to lengthen the timeframe for your least important debt to give you room and breathing space to tackle the ones that are creating the biggest problems for you and bring you back on track with your basic needs.

The easiest way overcoming new bad debt is to stay focused on your objectives. We have covered how money mastering begins with setting goals within your reach and working towards achieving them. But along that journey, you need to learn not to crave someone else's burger and fries while you're eating a salad. You need to learn to enjoy every bite of it because that's what's on the plate in front of you and that's what you have to work with. Satisfying your craving when it's out of your financial reach will only hinder your progress and knock you off the money mastering journey. There are so many other options, but you need to start actively asking yourself what else you could do instead of falling into the trap of just doing it without thinking.

For example, wouldn't it be a wiser option to save up for a short period of time to buy something you can't afford at that moment? Or wouldn't it be even better to properly budget through the month to avoid using your credit card to pay for things you don't have the cash for now? Your credit card should be there in case of any emergencies or unforeseen costs if you don't have an emergency fund in place. Incurring more debt on your credit card may limit your chances to save for any financial goals. If taking control of your finances is important to you, then you need to learn to stop using your credit card or credit cards unnecessarily. Hide them away if you can't curb your temptation to spend and see what it feels like to not have to pay that hefty instalment at the end of the month. Use that extra cash to open a short-term savings account and add money into it whenever you can as a backup for when you need it. The only reason why we have credit cards is to be able to pay when debit cards are not accepted – for example, renting a car. And whenever we use the credit card, we repay it in full the next month by planning for it and including it in our 50% necessities bucket before we even use the credit card to make the payment – no monthly instalments, no carrying over debt into the future. All gone because we budget and plan for it, whereas most people only repay the minimum amount (if at all). And if you don't really need a credit card, close it because the temptation will be always there.

Ultimately, debt and how you manage it is all about your priorities in life. We particularly like this Instagram image by a 26-year-old woman from the UK[viii]. She uses her Instagram profile to share her story of becoming debt-free and it's refreshing to see such a young person putting this much thoughtful effort into it. It's something we should all aspire to. An activity she does are no spend days and tracks them monthly in her profile, sharing with her followers. It's a great challenge to have if overspending is an issue for you that gets you into more debt and even better when you share it because that keeps you more accountable.

When it comes to debt, sometimes all is needed is to start adding a little extra payment to one debt monthly at a time. You can achieve this by reducing your monthly expenses which can be done in so many subtle ways if you simply work on changing your spending habits as we've discussed in previous chapters. Sacrificing a bit of your 20% fun bucket will help you pay the debt off quicker. Be consistent with payments and don't go back and forth with paying and spending on other things but stick to your monthly budget and your debt plan as part of it. This will allow you to start allocating more and more to this one debt. Discipline is what's required and as you get better at tackling one debt, you can move on to the next one and it'll be much easier. Using technology can help you make this as simple as possible through automatic transactions that go out on a pre-defined date with a pre-defined amount. And if you ever get a larger sum of money than the usual monthly instalment – through tax refund or side income – you can use it to speed up your debt repayments.

There are also other ways of reducing debt. Something as basic as turning off a light when you leave a room will eventually have a direct impact on your utility bill. Change your globes from regular to energy savers. Showering instead of bathing will reduce your water consumption which translates to a lower utility bill. Making lunch to take to the office instead of buying expensive takeout will make a tangible difference to your monthly expenses and to your health as well. Subtle changes can have dramatic results over time. It's all about priorities and having the right mindset. Money mastering just means being open and honest with yourself about the status of your financial health, identifying where changes can and need to be made, putting a strategy in place to achieve those goals, and diligently following it for as long as necessary without giving up or doubting your success.

Once you have settled a particular debt and the amount that you have consistently been allocating to that debt becomes cash flow, don't be tempted into spending it unnecessarily. It might be an idea that on the first month following a debt being settled and the account being closed that you take the amount that you would have spent on that debt and spoil yourself. We all deserve rewards for achievements that require consistency. Treat yourself to a day out with friends or buy yourself something you have had your eye on because you have come a long way. Thereafter, in the months that follow, allocate that instalment amount to another debt, split it across several debts, invest it, or save it for your emergency fund or next holiday since you're accustomed to already having it as a part of your budgeting plan. Eventually, you will reach a point where your bad debts are settled and without even knowing it, you'll have money available to channel into other objectives and priorities. Whatever you decide, remember the principle of settling your most expensive debts first is key to money mastering. And don't forget that it's not your debts with the highest amount outstanding, but rather your debts with the highest interest rates.

In summary, these are the key points around tackling debt:

- We live in a world where debt is almost unavoidable as financial institutions have found easy ways to trick us into spending money we don't have – for example, by using credit cards.

- Most people fall into debt because of bad spending like large purchases they cannot afford as well as borrowing money from different sources to live a lifestyle beyond their means (and often needs).

- Most people can't get rid of debt because of a lack of planning and a lack of consistency required to be successful especially because they have to sacrifice for a while.

# TACKLING DEBT

- Worst of all, most people forget that every time they incur credit card debt or any other debt, it is payable over time BUT with an interest rate, so they are losing money having to pay it.

- List all your debt and categorise it into good (debt that can bring you a return) and bad (debt that has no return), including total amount, interest rate percentage and timeframe. Prioritise it based on where you pay the highest interest rate and the importance for you.

- Regardless of which category they fit in, make sure you have them as part of your monthly budget within your 50% necessities bucket to pay the minimum amount required as you don't want to miss payments and accumulate more interest. But if have a lot more debt, then you might have to sacrifice your 20% fun bucket and your 30% future bucket for a while. Ideally, automate these payments as well so you don't miss any.

- After that, select the most important debt to you and review your spending to start allocating more money every month to repaying this debt through automatic deposits so you're covered – again, sacrificing your 20% fun bucket for a while might be smarter choice in the long run. Do this one debt at a time and as you progress, begin removing more, focus on your emergency fund and savings and on enjoying a less stressful life by achieving your financial goals.

- As you get better at managing debt, try to ensure it's part of your 50% necessities bucket.

- Track your progress monthly and celebrate every time you repay a debt in full because this will motivate you to continue going.

# TACKLING DEBT

# CHAPTER 7
# GROWING YOUR SAVINGS

Being in control of your finances means thinking about the future as well. As you become better at managing your monthly budget, tackling your debt, and saving money for emergencies, you can start thinking about how you can save more money to allocate for the future. Saving money can be one of the best financial habits you can adopt.

In this chapter, we will talk about why your 30% future bucket matters and how you can get to it by saving.

**The What**

Saving is money you set aside after paying all your expenses and covering necessary debt. It's money you don't spend but allocate for the future. Saving is about building assets. It's basically income not spent and it's the opposite of immediate consumption. Growing savings involves reducing expenditure and allocating leftover money as well as money from additional income sources (like passive income) to future use.

In addition to an emergency fund which we covered in Chapter 5, many save for a house, a car, a big wedding, children, vacations etc. All of these involve bigger sums of money than what you can cover with your usual monthly income. Often, people leverage special savings accounts, which is a service many banks offer so you can accumulate savings while generating interest on your deposits.

The key difference between saving and investment is risk. When you save, there's less risk involved because you have more control, unlike investment which is typically riskier due to outside factors you have little control over. Saving also means you have the money available when you need it, whereas with investment you need to sell your assets first before you realise a gain that you can use for any type of purchases. Saving is about keeping your money safe without that much return. With investing, on the other hand, your intent should be to make more income over time, meaning get a bigger return than the initial money you put in. All in all, saving is better used for short or mid-term needs, whereas investment should be long term.

The key saving categories you will often see are:

- Emergency fund – extensively covered in Chapter 5.

- Retirement funds – which we will talk about in Chapter 9 but in general, this is about securing your quality of life once you stop working.

- Irregular expenses – this covers bigger annual fees or taxes that don't fall into your usual monthly budget such as homeowner tax, insurances, annual car inspections, birthdays, or any type of presents for family and friends.

- Short-term to mid-term goals – these could include vacations, home purchases etc.

- Personal needs – anything you have to plan for beyond your usual monthly expenses such as new clothes, school fees etc. These are often called sinking funds.

Being clear on what you need to save for is the first step to mastering the growth of your savings.

## The Why

Regularly saving in addition to gathering your emergency fund and tackling debt is key to achieving financial stability. Although it's increasingly difficult to set money aside to save, it's a sure way of putting you in a better position later in your life and reducing worries.

When was the last time you laid awake in bed at 2 in the morning, wondering how you would get the money for something you need? We've all been there. It can be a stressful situation, draining you of your energy and ability to think clearly. Perhaps you were worried about how to pay your bills the next month, how to afford school supplies and books for your child, or how to afford to go to your brother's wedding. Money can be short as there is so much that we need and want nowadays. These things are not always emergencies so using your emergency fund for them is not an option. However, the same principles apply to generating other savings.

Saving is worth the effort even when you think you're barely managing to pay your bills because it can give you peace of mind. The only thing it takes is to start. Just €5 a week can make a difference because getting in the habit of doing this changes your outlook and perspective. Saving becomes easier the more conscious effort you put into it and without realising, you begin to accumulate more and more savings as your brain starts automatically making savings decisions. Everyone wants more money, but it's only those who work hard at saving that get it.

As you learn to manage your finances in a more sensible and strategic way and continue your path to financial wellness, you will also find that you begin to come up with other ideas on how to save money or how to create an additional income source. The thing with positive behavioural changes of any nature is that once you start to practice them, they have a ripple effect and overflow into other areas of your life. Financial distress without a strategy is like a dark cloud hanging over your head, but once you start taking the necessary steps to remedy the situation, you would see the positive light at the end of the tunnel. This is because your outlook has pivoted to positivity as you begin to worry less about your finances when your ideas and strategies are growing, ultimately improving your quality of life.

Saving means more control. When you have money allocated for various needs that you can tap into, you have options. When you don't have the money, you're stuck. Money doesn't solve every problem, but it does allow for more flexibility giving better chances at fixing the issue. For example, say you hate your current job. If you have money set aside, you can then focus on reskilling to change your career direction and invest more time in preparing for your next move without worrying about how you make the month. Being able to 100% focus on your new career goal in a stressfree way improves your chances of achieving it because the only thing your brain is working towards is this goal.

Ultimately, saving allows you to achieve the goals we discussed at the beginning of this book. Maybe you're planning for a major event in your life – like the big wedding you've always wanted. Or perhaps you want to buy a holiday home abroad and need to save the money for the down payment. Or you want to do a home renovation and build a new kitchen or purchase a new, bigger car to fit your growing family. Maybe you're also worried about how you will afford your child's education in the future. These are all very personal choices that require more money and saving is a way to help you get there without having to incur new debt. The sooner you start allocating a specific amount each month, the faster you'll achieve your goals.

Another benefit of saving is how it allows you to have more fun. Enjoying life now is so important because you don't know what can happen tomorrow. But without the money to do so, it can be frustrating. Saving allows you to afford this great holiday you've been dreaming about for a while or do a shopping spree without the feeling of guilt or getting yourself into debt.

In addition to the benefits of saving for the future, reassessing an impulse purchase you want to make now also helps you decide whether it's something you really need. Often, you realise it's something that won't make you any happier and avoiding wasting money on it instead of regretting the item after buying it was the better option. This is especially true as you start seeing your savings grow. And if the purchase is something you really need, then saving for it has the added benefit of accumulating interest on your deposits. This is by far the better decision than using your credit card to make the purchase right away and only incur more debt with more interest to pay. If we look at the household saving rate during the COVID pandemic, it rose significantly because people didn't have the opportunity to spend as much[ix]. This means that if you create barriers to spending, you can't have other excuses for why you're not able to save.

## GROWING YOUR SAVINGS

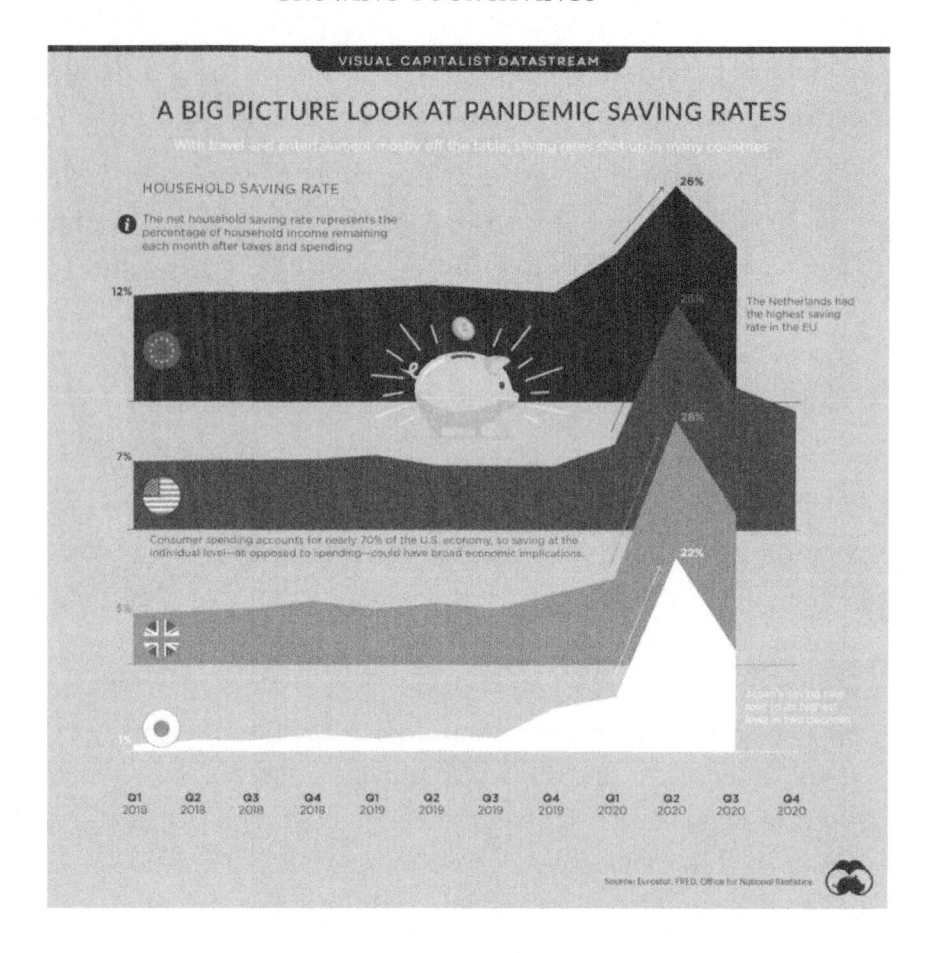

**VISUAL CAPITALIST DATASTREAM**

### A BIG PICTURE LOOK AT PANDEMIC SAVING RATES

With travel and entertainment mostly off the table, saving rates shot up in many countries

**HOUSEHOLD SAVING RATE**

The net household saving rate represents the percentage of household income remaining each month after taxes and spending

The Netherlands had the highest saving rate in the EU

Consumer spending accounts for nearly 70% of the U.S. economy, so saving at the individual level—as opposed to spending—could have broad economic implications.

Japan's saving rate rose to its highest level in two decades

Source: Eurostat, FRED, Office for National Statistics

Finally, if you have savings set aside, you're in a much better position to help others. This can mean helping through sponsoring charities or doing volunteering events or it could mean helping other family members in need. It's proven scientifically that it's not what we buy that makes us happy for the long term, it's giving back. Helping others also increases our sense of purpose in life[x].

If over time, you continue to grow your savings as well as invest, you might even be able to retire early and live off that money for the rest of your life without having to work. This is the ultimate dream for many, but it takes conscious effort and hard work to get there. For some, it might take 10 years, for others 40, but leveraging the compounding benefit of saving should be without a doubt a priority for you.

## The How

There are a few ways you can approach saving. What's truly key, though, is that your savings are aligned to your goals. When you're putting your budget together and you're planning how to structure your 30% future bucket, revisit the objectives you set up at the beginning of this book. You can set up a savings goal for each of them by calculating how much you need and by when, then divide that amount by what you need to save monthly. We mentioned that we usually look at saving in the following categories:

- Emergency fund – extensively covered in Chapter 5, which really is your number one priority when you start saving.

- Retirement funds – we will talk about this in Chapter 9 as this is about securing your quality of life once you stop working and it could be a mix of saving as well as investing.

- Irregular expenses – this covers bigger annual fees or taxes that don't fall into your usual monthly budget such as homeowner tax, insurances, tax on savings (yes, you should check if you have to pay yearly taxes on the amount of money you have in savings accounts) and birthdays, or any type of presents for family and friends. These always come up, so you need to plan for them

- Short-term to mid-term goals — these could include vacations, home purchases etc. based on what you hope to achieve in the next few years.

- Personal needs or sinking funds — anything you have to plan for such as new clothes, school fees etc. that your monthly budget can't cover.

The key difference between an emergency fund and a sinking fund is that emergencies are unplanned whereas the expenses that fit into your sinking fund are planned or at least you're aware that the probability for them to happen is quite hight.

To ensure we are not mixing up the money that is supposed to be allocated to different categories or items within them (like short-term to mid-term goals), we have set up different savings accounts and have automated the monthly deposits to go there as soon as we get paid so we don't have the temptation of spending that money. This is what people usually call 'pay yourself first'. Doing it this way allows you to also have a clear view of how you're doing on each of your saving goals for these key areas. Ideally, you should look for savings accounts that offer the highest annual or quarterly interest as possible, even though due to the COVID pandemic many banks significantly reduced the interest they pay. You also have two options with the savings accounts — flexible accounts where you can take out money anytime you want and so a lower interest rate or term deposits where you choose a timeframe during which you cannot touch the money you've deposited in and so a higher interest rate. The longer the timeframe, the higher the interest rate, but you need to be absolutely sure you will not need this money if you choose to go this way. But any money that is free is good and the longer you have funds in savings accounts, the more interest you will accumulate and the more the power of compounding will work wonders for you (provided inflation doesn't eat it up which is why we only recommend saving for mid-term goals as maximum length). Something worth repeating is that when you open new savings accounts, ensure that the bank's policy will cover you and know up until what amount in case they go bankrupt as you should not be taking risks with your savings.

When it comes to the frequency of savings transfers, you can opt for weekly, monthly, or quarterly interval savings deposits according to your budget. We tend to do monthly for regular savings and then one-offs for any additional income that we can allocate to our savings.

If breaking your savings into multiple categories is difficult for you, especially in the beginning, another way to think about it is to break your 30% future bucket into three:

1. 10% goes for short-term saving and sinking funds
2. 10% goes for mid-term saving
3. 10% goes for investments.

This is just an example and ultimately, you're the only person in the best position to decide how to allocate the money you want to save. And if you start with just one savings account, that's also fine. The sooner you do this and revisit your expenses to find ways to cut on them and allocate money in your savings account, the better. No matter how little you manage to save at first, with time it accumulates and amounts to bigger returns if you keep at it diligently. You also find more creative ways to improve your savings structure and amounts because you've been programming your brain to think in this direction more strategically. But make sure that when you start you aim to save an amount that is realistically achievable without overcommitting yourself as this could have the opposite effect of frustrating you. You need to set yourself up for success which is why budget management and journaling spending is so important.

We've covered reducing expenses a lot in Chapter 5 and Chapter 6, so the same principles apply, especially if you're currently not saving any money. You need to draw up your list of expenses from your journal to figure out how much you are spending during the month. Write everything, including the morning coffees that you buy, the bills you pay, your debt, groceries, emergency fund or anything else you spend on. If by looking at your spending and financial commitments you can't find anything left to allocate to savings, then try to find ways to decrease your usual spending. Identifying where you may be overspending and making conscious decisions to stop will help you put money aside for savings, no matter how little. Then set a reachable savings goal. Motivate yourself and commit to your goal without swaying.

And if starting with your big goals and sinking fund is too much for you, then think of something small – like a new pair of shoes you want to buy. Let's say they cost €90 and you don't have the money for them now. But you really want to have them, so you decide that within three months you will purchase them. This means you will need to save €30 per month which is €7,50 a week or approximately €1 per day. Breaking it down into small chunks makes it much more achievable. Now get a bottle or a box, make a small hole in it and every day put a 1-euro coin into it. Do this for 90 days consistently and you will get your shoes.

This principle is so simple but sometimes what's needed is to get in the habit of it and then planning for the bigger items becomes a lot easier.

If you find it difficult to save in addition to covering your monthly commitments and debt as well as building an emergency fund, think of ways to generate additional income. This can be done in several ways and forms and with the digital world at our fingertips, the process of getting started is simpler. A side hustle can generate an additional income source to use for saving. You could do online surveys for a few hours a day – there are plenty of sites depending on the country you live in. You could also offer your freelance skills (writing, video editing etc.) on websites such as Fiverr or Upwork. Etsy is very popular as well to sell various things you can make with your hands or Facebook Marketplace is your first go-to to sell items you no longer want. To be able to do this, you need to be creative and invest the time in the beginning.

Passive income is another way to general additional funds that has become quite popular in recent years. It's basically finding ways to make money with minimal effort. It's about monetising something that is non-revenue generating and converting it into a revenue generator. A good example could be your own website if you choose to use services such as Google AdWords and allow adverts on your site to pop up – when people click and purchase, you make a bit of money. It's the same with affiliate marketing, which is using links to promote services and products of other companies and if people click and purchase, you get money. Running a YouTube channel with a big following and enough advertising will help you make some money as well – there are even people who live off that completely, but it does involve your time and effort. Writing and selling a book is passive income as well. If you have a car, you can use it to advertise for companies. This will involve getting it wrapped in the company brand and you thereafter getting paid to just drive around and let people see the branding. The idea is that the more you drive, the more people get to see the advert so the more income you get. It requires minimal effort on your part and all you need to do is enquire with companies about branding your car. If you have a property to rent, that's also considered passive income, although it involves dealing with the people you rent it to, maintenance etc.

Before you embark on any sort of passive income generator, make sure you have thoroughly researched the side hustles of your choice to establish if this is, in fact, where you want to be investing your time and effort. The number one rule when you are looking at generating passive income is not to put yourself into debt in the process. At the outset, look at something that requires no financial investment from you and once that starts to generate an income, then you can begin considering other options.

In summary, here's how you should approach growing your savings:

- Revisit your goals and current spending alongside what you've decided to allocate to your emergency fund and clearing debt. If you're good on these two, establish what else you can redirect to additional savings.

- Allocate your 30% future bucket (without forgetting investment, which comes in the next chapter) around your goals, sinking fund and irregular expenses and how much weekly, monthly or quarterly you need to allocate for each of these.

- Decide on the appropriate saving tool based on what you want to save for – choose savings accounts that will work best for you when saving towards your goals. Study all your options to earn interest before choosing as you may miss an opportunity that could benefit you. Consider what option is best for your short-term and mid-term saving goals to choose the right savings account but always strive for the banks that give you the highest interest.

- Automate your savings transfers by choosing an option whereby your allocated amount for saving is deducted from your account automatically as soon as you get paid so you don't notice the money being deducted. Treat savings as paying a bill and forget about it at least for a while.

- If you're struggling to save anything, look at ways to build additional passive income. Be mindful that this involves time and effort to create, so it's not all free.

- Track how you're doing on your savings and whether you can increase more or adjust based on how you progress and your goals. Make saving a habit and be proud of how you're discovering more ways to get better at it, no matter how small the savings amounts are at the beginning.

# GROWING YOUR SAVINGS

# CHAPTER 8
# INVESTING

Warren Buffet – known as the "world's greatest investor" – whom we've already quoted a few times, once said that *"The best investment you can make is an investment in yourself... The more you learn, the more you'll earn."* This is particularly true when it comes to growing your money through investing. The more you know, the better you get at it (unless you make some very bad choices along the way).

In this chapter, we will cover what investing is, types of investments, why investing matters and why it differs from saving and we'll give you some tips on how to get started especially with investments in the stock market. A quick disclaimer before we get into it: we're not financial or investment advisors, just two ordinary people who have spent time learning about investing. Anything you read here is our knowledge but it's not financial or investment advice. It's your decision and responsibility whether you will invest your assets, money and resources in any shape or form, taking a potential risk, and if you do so, it's all up to you how you manage your investments moving forward.

### The What

When it comes to personal finances, investing is using your money to buy assets that increase in value over time and give you a return in the form of income. Successful investing is when you buy an asset at a low price and then sell it at a higher price, making a positive return on the difference called capital gain. This increase in value between the time you buy and the time you sell an investment is known as appreciation. You also generate income when you buy and hold investments without selling them through stock dividends that companies issue.

Let's look at the key investment types.

## Stocks

Companies sell stock to raise funds for their operations and future growth. If you buy stock from a company, you become a partial owner – called a shareholder – and you participate in the company's gains as well as losses. Some businesses pay dividends to their shareholders. Dividends are small payments on a regular basis, typically quarterly, for the trust and investment given.

Buying stocks can be risky because you cannot see the future and as much as a business has positive projections for its performance, you never know when the next COVID pandemic or global financial crisis might hit and whether the company would go bankrupt. Buying and holding stocks instead of selling is what many individuals do to avoid immediate losses and give the market time to recuperate. This is especially the case if you're not a professional investor whose job is to buy and sell daily to make a profit.

## Bonds

When companies and governments need to raise funds, they can borrow money from you as an investor. Essentially, businesses and countries issue debt, called bonds, and you can loan them money for a certain period to cover that debt. What you gain from doing this is a fixed rate of return as well as your original loan amount. Bonds are less risky than stocks because they guarantee a fixed income return but this doesn't mean that bonds are safe.

## Commodities

Commodities include physical products like agricultural goods such as wheat, energy products such as oil and metals such as gold, silver, etc. These are usually raw materials companies need in the production of end goods. The price for commodities depends on the demand for them in the market – take oil for example that's been becoming more and more scarce and so more and more expensive. This type of investment is considered high risk so best reserved for experienced investors.

## Real estate

Typically, real estate investments – houses, apartments, business units, land etc. – are assets whose value normally increases over time (unless we are in a financial crisis). We don't have experience in property (apart from our own house) but it's something we find very interesting because it suits our lifestyle and future goals. People buy property to rent and make an additional monthly income from that rent. Holiday properties can be particularly lucrative. However, investing in property is only an investment if you don't have to put yourself into more debt that you can't pay. If you do your math and can budget an additional mortgage that you can cover with the profit you will make from the rent and have something left for you, then that can be a smart move. Owning a property has added costs that you need to consider as well – transfer fees, registration costs, municipal fees, taxes etc. Especially important are the maintenance costs because if something breaks or requires repairs on a property that you are renting out, those costs will be passed on to you as the owner. Having property also requires time to manage the people who come in and rent, any issues they might have, all the communication with them etc. It can be time-consuming, and you need to factor this in because it's not always as passive and effortless as many believe it is. Of course, you can always hire a rental agency to manage all of this for you. Another interesting idea is to rent out a garage for storage. In recent years, this has become a very popular passive income generator because if you already own a garage that you don't use, it can be a very easy way to monetise it, especially because the time and effort involved to manage such a venture is not that high.

## Mutual funds and exchange-traded funds (ETFs)

These funds buy different combinations of the previous four investment types – stocks, bonds, commodities, and property. When you buy these, you invest in dozens or hundreds of different assets grouped together in a single fund which allows you to diversify your investment portfolio. This makes mutual funds and ETFs less risky than individual stocks. The difference between the two is how they are managed. Mutual funds have an investment professional who decides what assets to invest in on a frequent basis and by doing so, they try to beat a certain benchmark for performance. Because of this active management, mutual funds are more expensive to invest in than ETFs which are generally considered passive because instead of trying to beat a certain benchmark index, they try to copy its performance. ETFs are often the recommended investment type for beginners.

## Cryptocurrency

Cryptocurrency or often called crypto is a form of currency that exists digitally or virtually and uses cryptography to secure transactions, making it almost impossible to counterfeit. Cryptocurrencies are basically digital assets based on a network that is distributed across many computers and are not issued by any central authority, so they exist outside the control of governments. Most crypto is based on blockchain technology and it's become attractive because it has created a payment system that doesn't rely on banks to verify transactions. Many people believe that crypto will disrupt several industries and the biggest cryptocurrencies such as Bitcoin, Ethereum, Litecoin etc. have proved quite successful to early investors who have bought crypto. We still think investing in cryptocurrency is very risky as there are so many unknowns about it.

## Other types of investments

Staying on top of what's happening in the world, helps you identify other areas where you can invest money now and get returns later. Electricity prices have risen significantly in recent years due to the energy crisis we're in. Your electricity bills have surely been going up for quite some time and the price for petrol as well when you tank your car. Because of this and because we drive electric cars, we've invested in solar panels as it makes sense to our situation. We now produce our own energy at home which has contributed to a much lower electricity bill (or sometimes money back) and we don't pay as much at gas stations anymore.

## Investment in you

Investing is also about spending time and money to improve your life and the life of others. The first investment that Iliyana ever made was eye surgery. From a young age, Iliyana had to start wearing glasses. Every year, her sight would get worse, and she had to constantly buy new glasses and different types of lenses that she never managed to get used to. After she moved to Ireland, it took her one year to save remaining focused on her objective. She went and had the surgery, took a taxi back home, had a long afternoon and night sleep and woke up the next day seeing perfectly without glasses for the first time in many years.

Weeks after the surgery, she was still reaching for the glasses on her night cabinet that were no longer there. You might think this is not an investment but investing in you is the most important decision you'll ever make.

Some people throw themselves into investing without knowing some key pieces of information. Taxes are often overlooked. Depending on where you live, you will be paying different types of taxes for your investments or better said, for the assets that you own and sell. Most often, you pay capital gains tax on the money earned from selling anything on the stock market – the amount you sold for minus the amount you originally bought at is what you get taxed on. The percentage of capital gains tax is different in different countries so there's no set rule here but it can be quite high – in Ireland, for example, you pay 50% capital gains tax on your profits meaning you lose half of what you make (no surprise we moved away, right?). The Netherlands, for example, have a very different way of doing this – you pay a certain amount of taxes on simply owning assets in terms of savings and investments, basically on your wealth. Other countries don't have that at all and only tax you on the profit you make. Most people are afraid of taxes because they can get complicated, so you need to do your research. We have a tax accountant who helps us – we prefer to pay a bit for this than try to research this on our own in depth. But that's because we find the Netherlands complicated when it comes to taxes, maybe because we're expats here. Bulgaria, on the other hand, has much simpler rules (and way lower taxes) but we're not residents there. All in all, don't be afraid of taxes and don't have taxes stop you from investing. The main point here is that you need to be well informed to make good decisions that concern how much you invest now and what you expect to gain in the future having considered the taxes that you might have to pay along the way.

## The Why

Typically, inflation rises about 2% every year in most global economies, unless we face some type of a crisis of which we've had plenty in recent years. In 2022, inflation has been in the range of 7-10% in most global economies. In April 2022, inflation reached 9.6% here in the Netherlands[xi] (similar numbers in many other developed countries) meaning that just living here became 9.6% more expensive. We used to buy a kilo of chicken breast at our local market for €5.50 in December 2021, as of May 2022 a kilo of chicken breast at the same place costs €9.50. You do the math.

Inflation is the main reason we believe saving is best for short or mid-term goals and investment is where you put your money for the long term. The stock market typically beats inflation. The approximate average annual return of the S&P 500 index fund (an index of the 500 leading publicly traded companies in the United States) since its inception in 1928 through 31 December 2021 is 11.82%[xii]. Financial advisors will tell you to expect a typical average annual return of 7% for stock market investments. The stock markets are also cyclical depending on what's happening in the economy right now as the below image shows[xiii] but they usually always bounce back after a tough period. This means you can never really predict when a good time is to invest or to sell but you can at least have an idea depending on what's happening in the global economy.

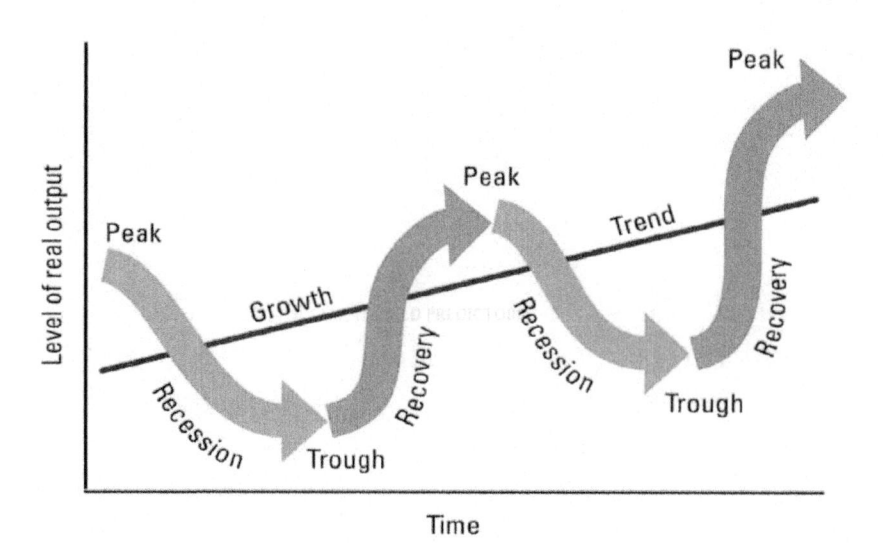

**The Economic Cycle**

There's also a fine balance between savings and investments. People will tell you different things, but we believe you should have a mix of the two. Savings certainly for your short and mid-term goals and investments for your long-term goals. Why is that? Anything shorter term is not worth the investment because you won't accumulate as much, you might even lose depending on how the market performs and you'll pay taxes. There's no point in investing your money when you plan to take it out in a few months or a few short years. Better save them. But for the long term, it's much wiser to invest than just saving because over the long-term your money loses its value due to inflation. Taking again the example of how life became 9.6% more expensive here in the Netherlands in April 2022, money in savings accounts didn't become 9.6% more valuable because the typical interest rate for savings accounts is just about 1% or less.

If your investments grow by 7% annually and inflation is 2%, then you've still grown your money by 5% unlike in a savings account where you might get an interest of 1% not allowing you to keep up with inflation. In addition, one of the powers of investing is compound interest which is often called "interest on interest". It means that you earn interest on both your initial investment as well as on the interest earned from the previous period.

Let's look at some example calculations to visualise this. There are a lot of calculators online and we've picked one from Fidelity[xiv] as it allows us to factor in multiple assumptions and clearly shows growth over time. For all examples, we will assume 2% inflation and a tax rate of 30%. These will vary per country, year, and economic situation so you can play around with the tool as well and calculate with different percentages for all of these. We will look at two examples – saving and investing with a different annual return as the main difference between the two. For both, we will also take two options – one where you increase your investment or saving amount as inflation increases and one where you keep your investment or saving amount static over the duration of the entire 10 years.

**Example 1**: Saving with a 1% annual rate of return for monthly deposits of $100 without initial investment for the duration of 10 years.

- Option 1: increasing saving amount annually to keep up with inflation – in this scenario, you put $10,796 into savings over the course of 10 years and only gain $527 on top of that.

## INVESTING

**In 10 years, your projected savings will be $11,323.**

- Amount invested — $10,796
- Simple earnings — $511
- Compound earnings — $16

Initial investment: $0
Time to grow: 10
Rate of return: 1.0%
Additional contributions: $100
Contribution frequency: Monthly
☑ Increase annual investment with inflation
Inflation rate: 2.0%
Tax rate: 30.0%

- Option 2: not increasing saving amount annually to keep up with inflation – in this scenario, you put $9.762 in savings over the course of 10 years and only gain $493 on top of that.

**In 10 years, your projected savings will be $10,255.**

- Amount invested — $9,762
- Simple earnings — $477
- Compound earnings — $16

Initial investment: $0
Time to grow: 10
Rate of return: 1.0%
Additional contributions: $100
Contribution frequency: Monthly
☐ Increase annual investment with inflation
Inflation rate: 2.0%
Tax rate: 30.0%

**Example 2**: Investing with a 7% annual rate of return for monthly deposits of $100 without initial investment for the duration of 10 years.

- Option 1: increasing investment amount annually to keep up with inflation – in this scenario, you put $10,796 into investments over the course of 10 years and gain $4,513 on top of that which is $3,986 more than Option 1 if you just save.

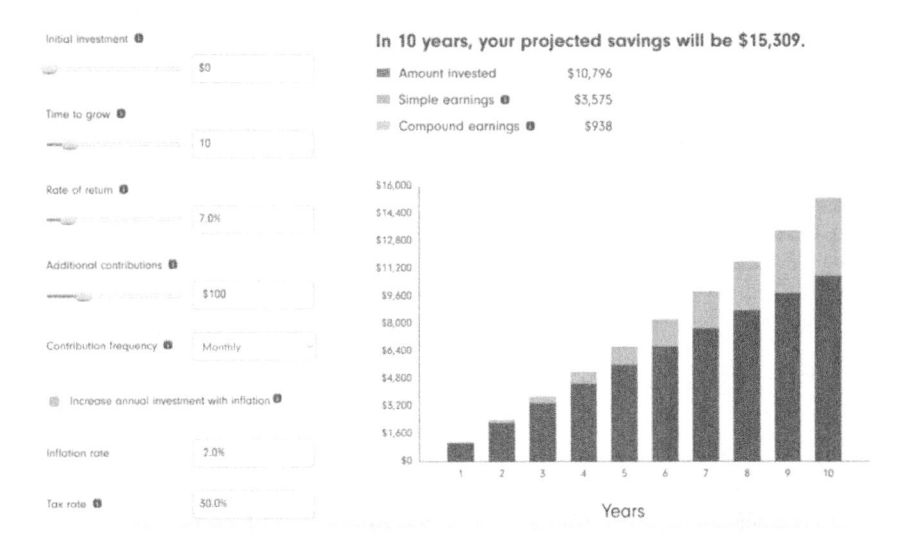

| | |
|---|---|
| Initial investment | $0 |
| Time to grow | 10 |
| Rate of return | 7.0% |
| Additional contributions | $100 |
| Contribution frequency | Monthly |
| Increase annual investment with inflation | ☑ |
| Inflation rate | 2.0% |
| Tax rate | 30.0% |

In 10 years, your projected savings will be $15,309.

| | |
|---|---|
| Amount invested | $10,796 |
| Simple earnings | $3,575 |
| Compound earnings | $938 |

- Option 2: not increasing investment amount annually to keep up with inflation – in this scenario, you put $9,762 in savings over the course of 10 years and gain $4,234 on top of that which is $3,741 more than Option 2 if you just save.

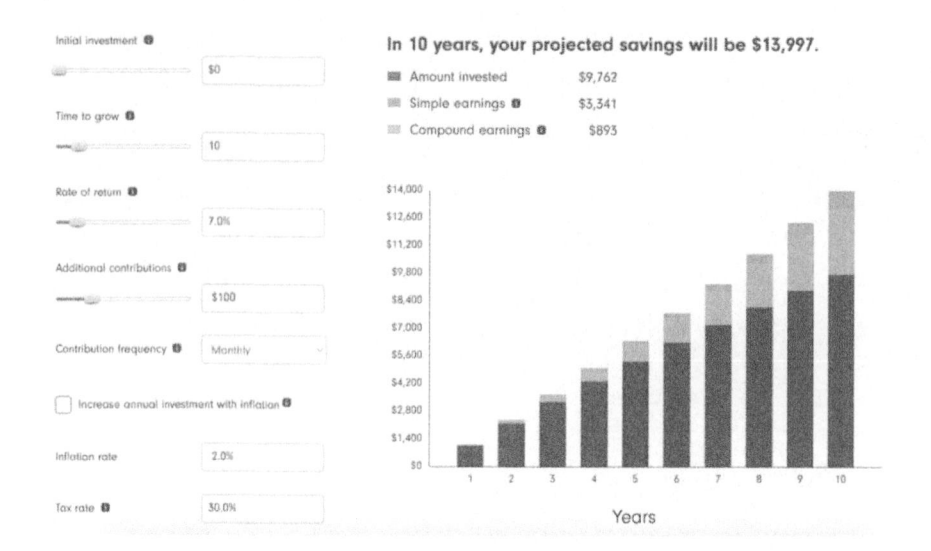

These examples give you an idea of what the return could be if you decide to invest rather than just save. Imagine what this could look like if you consistently invest for 30 or 40 years. The earlier you start, the better, no matter how small of an amount. Don't forget, though, that investing always has its risks. No one can guarantee you a consistent annual return of whatever percentage because we simply don't know what will happen tomorrow and so there's no way to predict how the market will perform either.

## The How

Before we get into the how, we want to first mention that in this section we will focus on giving you some basic tips about investing in the stock market. We are not financial or investment advisors so what will follow is foundational knowledge we've acquired. Still, it's your responsibility to continue researching and learning and it's up to you whether you will decide to invest or not. We don't have any responsibility for your decisions and actions you might take after reading any of the advice in this book.

When it comes to investing, here are the key rules you need to think about:

- Buy and hold
- Invest regularly
- Diversify your portfolio
- Stick to your strategy

We will talk about each of these rules but before that, you need to find a broker to be able to buy and sell on the stock market. A broker is an individual or a company who acts as an intermediary between you and the exchanges where the trading of stock happens. You always have the option to find someone else to invest on your behalf but that comes with its own risks and is typically more expensive as you need to pay fees and commission for the service. Nowadays, it's become a lot easier to do this on your own because you can leverage a trading platform where you create your personal account and you're given access to the stock exchanges to trade. You can do this on your laptop or often through an app on your phone depending on the broker and if they have one. When choosing an online broker or trading platform, you need to research their fees for making transactions, commissions they might be getting etc. as well as how big their portfolio is in terms of how much access to stocks and funds you will have available to buy from. It's never free but you can find brokers with very low fees and still relatively large investment options. Some of the most popular ones are eToro, Fidelity, Degiro, Morgan Stanley, and Charles Schwab. Some require an initial investment from you when you register whereas with others you can start with a very small amount when you're ready rather than immediately. Depending on where you live, you will have different trading platforms to choose from.

**Buy and hold**

As explained in this chapter so far, it's best to invest in the stock market for the long term. This is what people call "buy and hold" meaning invest now and don't sell. Wait it out because over time, your investments begin to generate a profit for you and it gets bigger thanks to compounding. When you start, you might want to pick low-risk stock at first such as ETFs rather than dive deep into buying certain company stocks that seem attractive. Whatever you decide to buy, make sure to do your proper research and consider any trading fees that you will have to incur for the transactions with your broker. If you're too worried about picking the wrong stock, you could start investing with a robo-advisor which are automated investment platforms that help you invest in already created and diversified portfolios based on your goals and how much risk you want to take.

**Invest regularly**

For the best compounding result, you should invest consistently, ideally monthly, and you should start now. Look at your budget and decide what type of monthly amount you can allocate to investments, no matter how small. This should be part of your 30% future bucket. As we've discussed, you could base how much you want to invest depending on your goals or just pick 10% of your future bucket to go to investments. If you can, set up regular, automatic transfers from your current account to your trading platform on the day you get paid as this should be a priority after tackling key debt and emergency fund savings. Create a recurring calendar appointment with yourself to trade monthly. Consistency is what allows you to grow your investments and ultimately take advantage of the compounding benefits we've covered. As your salary increases, make sure to increase your investment amounts proportionately as well. In addition, if you get dividends paid out – reinvest them instead of selling them.

**Diversify your portfolio**

To avoid risk, make sure you have different types of stock investments. You should ideally have a mix of ETFs or stocks from different industries. This is to ensure that if one industry, say technology, is going through a bad time, you won't be hit as hard because the other industries in your portfolio can offset this loss. Here again is where you need to be well informed and over time aim to build a better and more diversified portfolio of investments. This also applies to eventually having different types of investments – stocks, property, etc. Diversification is especially important to people with low-risk tolerance.

**Stick to your strategy**

Don't get scared of market fluctuations. Markets can be volatile, and we've already discussed that they have ups and downs periodically. When investing in the stock market, caution yourself against having unrealistic expectations of the performance of stocks. What many people do is sell their investments when they start seeing a dip. But if your goal is to build your own little fortune, then you need to understand that markets are cyclical. There will always be dips and you need to hold and wait them out because the market will go up again. They say there's a market crash or crisis every ten years. Stick to your strategy and goals and don't get in the habit of reviewing what's happening in your trading platform daily. This can only create worries especially if the market is down and you start seeing a loss in your portfolio. Keep the long-term view in sight and continue investing.

There are not always guarantees of high returns on investments and you could very well lose money if you don't make informed choices. Although there are benefits, there are also risks. However, the earlier you gain knowledge and start investing, the greater your chances are of maximising your return on investments given you know what you're doing. And if you're not yet in a position to start investing, use the time to educate yourself.

In summary, here's what you need to remember from this chapter:

- Investing is best as a long-term strategy and saving is better suited for short to mid-term goals. The main reasons for this are inflation, risk and benefit of compounding.

- Over time, inflation can eat up your savings and you may not get many returns, but investing can bring an average annual return of 7% and typically beat inflation also because of the power of compounding where you continue making profit not just on the original investment amount but on subsequent interest year after year.

- If you know you need to make a purchase in the short to mid-term, there's no point in investing your money and it's better to put it in a savings account. This is because the markets can be volatile and if you end up having to sell when the market is down, you may lose. In addition, you pay taxes for the profit you make when you sell stock so make sure you factor the amount depending on where you live.

- The most popular investment types are stocks, bonds, commodities, and property. Mutual funds and ETFs are indexes that group the above and are usually recommended for those just starting with investing.

- If you do decide to invest, pick the right trading platform (or a professional) based on fees, commissions, functionality, and investment options.

- Then remember the four key rules around investing: buy and hold for the long term, invest regularly as part of your 30% future bucket in your monthly budget, diversify your portfolio over time to avoid risk, stick to your long-term strategy and don't get bogged down when the market is not performing well – it will most likely get back up after a while.

- Keep learning and researching about the stock market and investments. Information is power and the more you know, the better and smarter decisions you can make, helping you avoid risk and losses.

# INVESTING

# CHAPTER 9
# GETTING READY FOR RETIREMENT

No one will tell you that getting old is sexy. Instead, there's a negative connotation with it because we immediately imagine sickness and the inability to do the same things that you do when you're young. But getting old is a natural part of life. The earlier you begin to financially prepare for your older age, the less stress you'll have when the time approaches. In addition, if you remain focused on all the money mastering tips we've given you so far in this book, you should be able to develop a different mindset around money to allow you to plan more strategically for the future. By doing so, you might find yourself in a situation where you can retire earlier and are still able to support the lifestyle you want to live. In this chapter, we will talk about the options you have to get ready for retirement – regardless of whether you want to do this at your retirement age or earlier.

**The What**

Retirement is when you reach the age specified by your country when you are no longer supposed to work. The typical retirement age in many countries is 65 but in recent years, the option to retire early and live off savings and investments has become quite popular, although not everyone manages to achieve this. Retirement is supposed to mean being financially independent to enjoy the lifestyle you want and celebrate all the years of hard work without having to work anymore.

The reality, though, is that few manage to live happily ever after work. We live much longer nowadays. State pensions are too low and life keeps getting more and more expensive. Some people end up continuing to work after retirement age to be able to cover their monthly needs. Other people rely on the help of their children.

Retirement is this uncertain time that you know is coming, but you don't think about it as it's too far away. Most of us are not informed well enough about what we get when we retire. Expecting that a state pension will cover you for the rest of your life is a mistake and not everyone has the benefit of having an employer-sponsored retirement plan that guarantees a source of income during retirement. Information and planning are key to ensuring you will have enough money to enjoy your life after years of non-stop working. If you want to live a certain lifestyle after retirement, then you might have to rely on your own savings and investments. In Western European countries, you will see lots of people relying on additional pension funds to not just plan for living comfortably after they retire but to plan for sickness and the need for medical assistance or special facilities so it's not their children who have to pay for these.

## The Why

The earlier in your career you start saving for retirement, the better. A major reason is that you give yourself a longer period to invest which results in a higher return but also ensures that you won't have to be putting away a very big sum if you start late. Whether we start saving for retirement at 20 or 40 years old, making the decision to put money away for when we can no longer work will guarantee that we don't become financial burdens to others. The thing is, if you're employed, no matter how high or low your salary is, putting a small amount away monthly will accumulate over the years and see you through retirement.

We've mentioned earlier that most people will outlive their savings by 8-20 years. What's also concerning is that the gap seems to be increasing for women. A picture speaks a thousand words, so looking at the below image of the analysis done by the World Economic Forum [xv] truly puts the gravity of the issue into perspective:

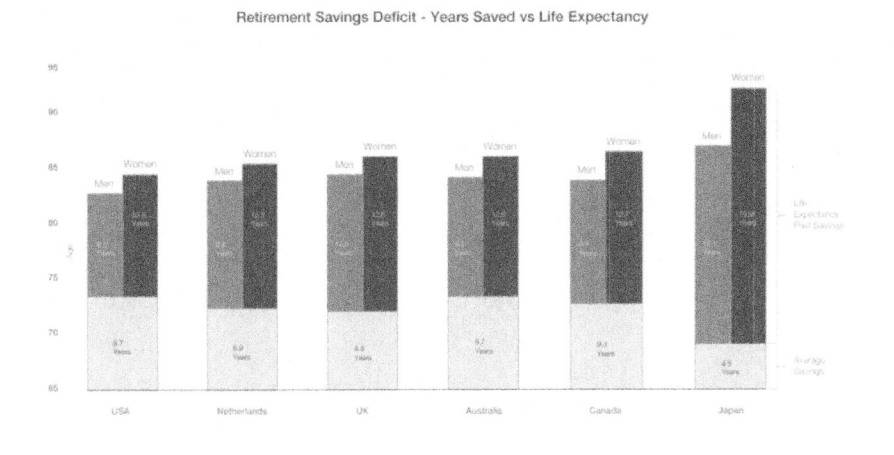

Retirement Savings Deficit - Years Saved vs Life Expectancy

Source: World Economic Forum Analysis

Here's how the World Economic Forum explains the problem:

*"Why are people outliving their retirement savings? Poverty has decreased just as medical advances and improved healthcare provision have increased.*

*Along with other factors like greater global awareness of the benefits of a healthy diet and regular exercise, this means people are living longer.*

*By the middle of this century the proportion of over 60s in the world's population is set to reach 22%* [xvi]*, almost double the 2015 figure, according to UN figures.*

*Our aging population has placed unsustainable pressure on government and employer-sponsored pension systems, leading to a growing trend for individuals to take responsibility for financing their own retirement. But savings have failed to keep pace with the decline in traditional pension plans, leading to the current retirement savings deficit."*

To explain the problem in clear numbers, the global gap between retirement savings and retirement income needs is projected to reach $400 trillion in three decades – more than five times the size of the global economy.[xvii]

Most people don't even think about this problem. It's too far out. A quarter of Americans for example have no retirement savings, zero[xviii]. Many of us live for the current moment and enjoy the fruits of our work now which is certainly fine. But we believe there should be a happy balance between the two – enjoy the now but prepare for the future.

What's the solution? Obviously, governments and companies have a lot of work to do, but it's also in your hands to prepare for retirement and not become affected by a gap of 8-20 years with no money to live off.

### The How

Typically, there are three ways to think about retirement and pensions:

- Government schemes
- Workplace pension schemes
- You own retirement investments

Government schemes vary considerably in different countries, which is why we cannot advise on what the best option is for you here, but we recommend you spend some time researching what the situation is in your country. Typically, state pensions are rather low, so you have to rely on workplace contributions and individual contributions or a mix of the two.

You should always take advantage of pension schemes offered by your company as this is a forced way of investing because the money is deducted off your salary before it hits your account. Company pension plans are typically based on your age, years of service with the company and your compensation. Through employer-driven pensions, you are not tempted to spend the money allocation as it is not a part of your monthly budget that is accessible. In addition, many companies offer to match your contribution, so if you decide to contribute 3% of your salary to your pension, then your company can also provide 3%. Depending on the pension scheme of the organisation where you work at, it's always a good idea to choose the maximum percentage. Some companies increase their contribution as your age increases as well. The money contributions usually go into a pension fund managed by a professional investment company. You can track how much you have now as well as the expected returns when you retire on their platform. Often, you can't touch this money until your retirement age. When you change jobs, though, ensure that you are not tempted to withdraw those funds like so many people are and end up paying a ton of taxes as well. What you should do instead is transfer your contributions to the fund your new company offers or let them remain in your previous fund if possible. Sometimes transferring might require paying taxes, so you should be mindful of the conditions. By withdrawing the funds, you are breaking the cycle of compound interest and have to start from scratch again with a new fund which is not a sensible financial decision.

The last option is to put aside money in your own investment fund as we've discussed in the previous chapter and do this for the long term until you retire. You can also look for specific pension plans that banks and insurance companies offer where you live. This is an easy way to begin investing for your retirement and often times the money gets invested for you depending on your goals and risk tolerance so you don't have to worry about where to invest. Before going this route, make sure to discuss all your options, including conditions such as potential fees, commissions to pay, your returns and interest rate etc. If you choose to save for your retirement on your own (or as an addition to government and work-related pension schemes), this should become part of your 30% future bucket.

### 20- to 30-Year-Olds

The first thing to consider is that the earlier you start investing, the better. If you start planning toward retirement from your first salary cheque, your monthly contributions will be lower than someone who starts years later. They would have to contribute a little more in order to achieve the same return on investment by the same retirement age. The reason for this is because of the power of compounded interest. Remember that when you start investing in your 20s, you have a lot more freedom as to how and where your money is invested because generally at this stage in your life there are no major life events taking place that you have to plan for financially. That is the beauty of investing early on in your career. Fewer responsibilities cut you slack to contribute larger amounts.

### 30- to 40-Year-Olds

If you're planning on starting to invest in your 30s, there are various factors to consider because this is the time when major decisions to buy a house, get married or have children are usually made. While it would have been great if you had started investing a bit earlier, don't be stressed that you didn't. There is no time like the present and as we've already said, the sooner you start investing, the better.

When you start investing in your 30s, you need to be realistic about what your goals are. Since you're probably just starting to think about buying your new house or getting married, making allowances for children and college funds is not necessary at this stage. Focus on your immediate needs in your current position and how that will play out financially by your planned retirement age. As your circumstances change and children arrive, you can start planning for the financial implications that come with those responsibilities. Without dependants, it's not necessary to have life policies in place yet, but that will change as your circumstances change.

Although you're only starting to invest in your 30s, the upside is that your earning potential should have grown substantially since your 20s which means you could be better placed financially to contribute a higher amount to your retirement. In addition, you still have a lot of years ahead of you before retirement which leaves plenty of room for your investments to grow and meet the needs you have in your mind of what income you want to be generating when you reach retirement.

## 40- to 50-Year-Olds

In this age bracket, things change substantially when it comes to investing. In your 40s most people are either married and have children or have heavy financial commitments. This means that these things need to be factored into your investment portfolio. Tertiary education is expensive and it's important to consider contributing toward an education trust for your children. This is also the age bracket where people become financially complacent because they have generally purchased a home and a car and for the most part are content. Most people in this age group are in a higher salary bracket and most of them have learnt to manage their finances sensibly and make financially sound decisions.

The problem with this age bracket is that because they are somewhat financially secure, they look at upgrading their house and car in line with their salary as opposed to increasing investments. Just because you can afford to buy a better car or house, doesn't mean you should if you don't have a retirement plan. If you have liquid cash and are happy with where you are living because it suits your needs and the car you are driving is reliable and often paid off by this stage, it doesn't mean that you can become complacent with how you spend your money.

You should, though, consider investing in policies that will protect your children and spouse, should you no longer be here. You need to ensure that you have adequate plans in place that would take care of your children and their needs until they are adults. Also, you would need to draft a will and nominate someone as Executor so that in the event of your untimely demise, your children will be taken care of financially.

Remember to be practical in the financial decisions you make at this point in life as building up your retirement fund should be of importance. This is the age bracket where you can start to take less calculated risks and think more about where to invest in a higher-risk portfolio which will provide higher returns on investment in the long run. Don't forget that to retire and maintain the same lifestyle that you are currently accustomed to, your retirement plan should most likely aim to pay you no less than your current annual salary.

## 50- to 60-Year-Olds

We have highlighted the fact that the earlier you start investing in your retirement the better, but that doesn't mean that if you're in your 50s and haven't adequately planned for your retirement that it's too late. The financial circumstances of a fifty-year-old often look very difficult to someone in their thirties. By this age, your children will most likely have finished school and will have become self-sufficient, which means that the money you were investing in an education fund for them can now be directed to an investment plan for yourself. You may have also built up substantial savings which you can redirect into more aggressive investment funds.

A further benefit is that by the time you are in your fifties, most people have reached the point where they are downsizing their lifestyle. They no longer need big family homes or big family cars and the expenses related to having those things. You may have been able to repay your mortgage as well so by downsizing to a new home and selling your current property which should have increased in value, you might be able to make quite a good return from the sale that can be reinvested for retirement.

You will need to remember to manage your risk strategically because your investments will be shorter term and should your investments not perform as planned, you have a shorter time to recover any losses. It might also be a good idea to seek professional help and leverage investment firms to increase the probability of reaching your retirement goals.

In summary, here's what you need to remember about preparing for retirement:

- Getting old may not be sexy, but it's a part of life and the sooner you start preparing for those years where you will no longer work, the more you'll be able to enjoy them.

- The first step you can take right away is to inform yourself about the government pension schemes in your country and how much you would expect to get from them. Second, review what your company offers as you may be able to max out your contributions if they offer you a pension plan and find out how much this could mean for you when you retire.

- Think about investing additional money as part of your 30% future bucket depending on your retirement goals. You can do this on your own as we've discussed in the previous chapter or rely on pension plans offered by a bank or an insurance company in the country where you live.

- Be aware that we often miscalculate how much money we will need for retirement because not only do we retire later, but we also live significantly longer which adds years to the amount of cover you will require to maintain the same lifestyle you are used to after retirement. Starting early is key to avoiding risk in the future or a situation where you don't find yourself with enough. The earlier you start, the less aggressive your contributions will need to be.

- Don't forget that life happens now. You should not sacrifice everything you have to prepare for the future because you never know what might happen tomorrow. Strive to find a healthy balance between now and the future.

# CHAPTER 10
# SUMMARY

*Rich people believe 'I create my life.' Poor people believe
'Life happens to me.'* – T. Harv Eker

Money mastering is all about changing your mindset. When you change your mindset, you can then change your habits. When you change your habits through regular practice, you create discipline. Discipline in thinking and doing will allow you to control your money and life rather than let money control your life.

In this book, we've laid out the foundational knowledge for managing your personal finances. We have shared multiple lessons in financial literacy that you should have been taught at school. Our advice is to take these tips bit by bit and make small changes but truly adopt them and make them stick. Progress over perfection should be your mantra.

In this last chapter, we will summarise some of the key learnings, ideas, and practical advice.

**Typical financial situations people get themselves into**

Look at your current financial situation and identify what might be creating problems for you. There are several elements of financial mismanagement that are easy to spot and remedy. The most common cause is overspending while other factors are subtle and creep up before you know it. This includes credit card debt and high-interest loans that become very difficult to pay back. Make the decision to work towards changing this behaviour. Ask yourself how you arrived at this distressful point with your

# SUMMARY

finances and what you can do to change it. Be honest with yourself – no one will judge you as this is your path to money mastering.

If loss of income is affecting you, you may need to create a plan to help you get out of this situation while looking for new work and maintaining your current financial commitments. Slimming down on spending is the best you can do, even if you have to sacrifice certain areas of your life for a while.

If you tend to overspend or make unnecessary purchases, challenge yourself as you give thought to what you have learnt so far. Don't be fooled by marketing adverts that catch your eye as it is a means to lure you and your credit cards into debt. Always shop with a list so you don't exceed your budget with unnecessary purchases or opt for online shopping if the temptation to spend unnecessarily is overwhelming. Reward yourself with a cheat day that has a capped budget at the end of each month, and you will be astounded by the results of how quickly you transition into a disciplined spender. The months that you decide to skip the cheat day, take the amount you were supposed to spend and place it in a transparent jar. Just like weight loss dieters measure their waist and use the centimetres they have lost as motivation, having a visual of the money you have saved will serve as fuel to aid in the continuation of your journey. When you do decide to reward yourself with a spending cheat day, use the money from that same jar to do so. Eventually, you will come to the decision of whether you want to see that jar full or empty.

If living off credit is your current lifestyle, you will need to ask yourself 'why'. How did you get here and why does it matter to you to continue living this way? If you're living beyond your means just to impress others, this is probably not the right way to look at your life as you'll be eternally stressed about money. First, you need to decide to make the change and prioritise what truly matters. Then you need to look at all your current debt and find ways to pay off the most expensive one first – the one with the highest outstanding interest rate – while still paying your other regular debt on time so you don't accumulate more. Keep building resilience and remember, it's not money you have earned, it's money you're borrowing.

**Blueprint for effective money management**

Financial plans are put in place to ensure you manage your money well. This means meeting both current and future financial commitments and goals. Our blueprint for effective money management consists of three key principles:

1. **Define your short-term, mid-term and long-term objectives.**

Make an appointment with yourself or with your partner and talk about the goals in your life. Do you want to travel the world? Are you planning a big wedding? Do you want to buy a property? Is retiring early a priority? Think about what you want to achieve in the next few months, a few years, and five years and beyond. Write these down as your goals with a timeline to achieve them. Having a list of your financial goals instead of keeping them at the top of your head is the first step to successfully reaching them. Lay your goals out logically so that you know what you want to accomplish and how you are going to accomplish it. Now plan how you can achieve these goals from a financial standpoint. Don't set unreachable expectations as it's a recipe for failure. If you have big goals, be prepared to wait out the length of time it takes to achieve them as patience is rewarding. Overwhelming yourself in the process will not help you achieve what you want. Start backwards by identifying how much you need for each goal, then think about a realistic timeline to achieve it and divide the total money needed by this timeframe to find out how much you would need to be separating for this goal monthly. This money might go into savings or investments depending on whether this is for the short, mid, or long term.

2. **Allocate the budget to cover them based on priorities.**

Once you have identified what you need to achieve your goals, start putting this into action by allocating the necessary budget for each of these goals based on what's your number one priority is. Have different savings and investment accounts so you don't mix up money that is supposed to go for different things. Your monthly budget should break down what's needed in the required amounts and as you hit a goal, reallocate the leftover money to the next goal.

3. **Automate everything, incl. savings and investments.**

The best way to ensure money goes into your goals is to automate all the payments. Remember the saying 'pay yourself first.' As soon as you get your salary, ensure you have automatic transfers going to savings or investment accounts. This way you don't even have the chance to spend the money because it's already gone to where it's supposed to. The rest is really what will go into your usual monthly spending and so you won't fall into the trap of saving what's left because there's never anything left. If there's money available, you will spend it.

As part of your blueprint, look at **creating and managing a budget**. This budget will help you allocate your money the right way every month. We recommend following the rule of 50-30-20:

- 50% of your money goes for basic necessities – this includes all regular expenses such as rent, mortgage, utility bills, insurance, groceries etc. and ideally all debt.

- 30% of your money goes for the future – this is where you think about savings and investments to hit your mid to long-term objectives and you build up an emergency fund.

- 20% of your money goes for fun – this includes going out for a drink with friends, buying some new clothes etc. This is important because you need to enjoy life and enjoying life happens now. But if you have too much debt, this is the bucket to sacrifice.

The way you make a budget work is through **journaling spending**. If you've never looked at where all your money goes, now is the time to start. This exercise can be eye-opening and help you spot activities or areas where you're overspending without even knowing. For the next three months, be very disciplined and track every expense – cash, debit card, or credit card. Write them down in an excel sheet or use one of the popular money tracking apps. Categorise your spending based on key categories like rent/mortgage, groceries, bills, debt, fun activities, savings, and investments, if any. Calculate how you spend against how much you've earned this month (expenses vs. income). Look at the gap and where you're overspending. Do this regularly – in the beginning, you may need to track daily and pivot as you spot issues. Make this an appointment in your calendar and at the end of the month review your entire spending and think about your commitments for the next month to identify what you can change.

As you get better at noticing where your money is going now, it's time to consider how you tackle the biggest and most important areas of a well-managed money plan:

**Contribute toward an emergency fund.** Unexpected emergencies are unavoidable, no matter how careful we can be. The reason behind saving for an emergency fund is to help you weather any storms that may unexpectedly come your way – COVID, illness, death of family members etc. To avoid any incurrence of debt when this happens, having an emergency fund is important. It's a means of aiding you in your time of need, so you don't have to reach out to your credit cards etc. and increase your debt amount. Aim towards saving three to six months of living expenses and make this a priority as part of your 30% future you bucket.

**Tackle debt** by developing a plan that cuts down on spending and increases monthly debt payments. Reassessing your budget is a very good way to get rid of accumulated debt and avoid you from incurring more debt in future. Debt should be quite simple actually – don't spend more than what you earn, but we know it's not always easy. Sometimes you have good debt (the one that can bring you a return like property) and other times you have bad debt (the one that doesn't bring any return at all and is more of a burden). List all your debt, including the total amount, date due, monthly instalment, and interest rate. Prioritise your debt based on where you pay the highest interest rate and if you have debt with an interest rate of 7% or more, aim to get rid of it as soon as possible. Sacrifice other buckets of your budget if necessary. Then tackle the other debts one by one based on priority.

**Save and invest in your future** by including a savings and an investment strategy into your financial plan and monthly budget. Open savings accounts to allocate money toward your short and mid-term goals as well as irregular big expenses and personal needs but choose to invest for your long-term goals, including retirement. This way, you ensure that your money doesn't get eaten up by inflation which is an unavoidable occurrence. You should have a good understanding of how investments (stock, bonds, commodities, real estate, mutual funds and ETFs, cryptocurrency etc.) work so that you know where your hard-earned cash is going because investing comes with risks. If you do decide to invest, remember the four key rules: buy and hold, invest regularly to benefit from compounding, diversify your portfolio to avoid risk, stick to your long-term strategy and don't sell because the market is down, wait it out. But if you have a lot of debt and no emergency fund to fall back to, saving and investing make no sense until you tackle the above two. Also, don't forget to invest in yourself, your skills, and your health because you're your most important asset.

**Preparing for retirement.** To retire comfortably without worrying about how you will survive after your working life has ended, you need to contribute to a retirement plan as early as possible. Inform yourself about the government and company-led schemes that exist in your country and contribute the maximum you can from your monthly salary. Then think about when you want to retire, what lifestyle you want to live then, and what the gap might be between what you'd get out of state and company-led pensions. Consider opening your own retirement fund and contributing to it monthly. Although you can start your retirement plan at any age, starting off earlier will avoid you from paying a bigger premium to reach a full retirement payment at the end.

In addition, insurance and medical policies are important because they cover you for circumstances you may not expect. They also ensure that you don't have to rely on your emergency fund or accumulate new debt. Nobody wants to think about the bad stuff like injuries or a fire in your house, but you never know what will happen tomorrow. Ensuring you have a plan to protect what you've been building should anything happen to your health, assets, or job is the smartest move you can take now.

# SUMMARY

Finally, get in the habit of **reviewing your budget, goals, and financial plan regularly**. Make this an appointment in your calendar monthly. Track how you're doing, where you can do better and most importantly, be proud of your successes, no matter how small. Make sure to note how much you have now in your saving, investment, and retirement funds so you can follow your growth over time and evaluate whether you're doing well against your goals.

The worse thing that you can ever do to injure your financial health is to lose sight of your goals. This will extend the time you take to eventually reach them which can be a major setback. Focus on your priorities and not on the temptations that lure you to spend unnecessarily. Don't allow anyone to steer you off your path. Once you embark on your money mastering journey, don't let those around you influence the positive decisions you are making. Remember, others have no idea what your financial goals are so stay focused and disciplined. Remember that being in financial distress has a direct impact on your emotional health as well. If you have a partner, being in financial distress can put massive, unnecessary strain on your relationship. Poor money management choices can have an adverse effect on your personal life. If you follow the practice of being truthful and collaborative with your finances, then this partner's marathon will be easily run. The effects of working together rather than secretly or against each other bear many fruits that you both can devour.

Remember that **practice creates progress** and things constantly repeated, whether good or bad, become habits. The first few days and weeks are always the most difficult. The key is to push through the difficult days until the old habits have been broken psychologically and replaced with new, healthy habits. They say it takes 21 days to form a habit. Once you have mentally overcome or broken the old habits, following your new way of life will get easier as time goes by. With time, practising the money mastering principles from this book will prove fruitful to those who are diligent and focused. It takes determination, consistent effort, patience, and time, but it's worth it. There's nothing more empowering that having control of your money and the freedom to do with it as you please.

Don't forget to count your wins, no matter how small, and celebrate when appropriate which doesn't always have to include spending more money. Be proud of yourself and share your successes with family and friends. Congratulate yourself on achieving what you set out to do and use this improvement as fuel and motivation to continue your journey. Remember, money mastering is a marathon, not a sprint.

# SUMMARY

# BONUS CHAPTER
# THE MONEY MASTERING CHALLENGE

We want to ensure that you put everything you've learned in this book into practice as soon as possible. This is why we've written this bonus chapter to give you some simple steps you can take to start mastering money now.

Follow this as guidance for every week of the month. Print this out if you want and strikethrough activities you have completed as well as write down what you've achieved, no matter how small. Every little win counts as progress.

**Week 1: Understand your financial situation**

The goal of this first week is to understand your current financial situation. You should aim to calculate the difference between how much you earn and how much you spend in a month. You need to create an initial view of what you're spending your money for through your first journal. List everything: things like monthly bills for your home, electricity, water, internet, phone etc., then for groceries and eating out in restaurants, debt on credit cards as well as loans from the bank or friends/family, daily coffees, drinks with friends, shopping for clothes etc. – absolutely everything you use your cards as well as cash to pay for within a month.

**Week 2: Identify your biggest financial problem right now**

In your second week, your objective should be to identify what's the biggest financial problem you're fighting right now. For most people, this is debt that you can't seem to be able to get yourself out of. List all your debt – bank loans, loans from friends/family, credit cards. Write down how much you still owe, when the due date is and how much the interest rate is for each debt. Prioritise your debt and decide which is the one debt that's creating the biggest issues for you and that you need to repay as soon as possible. This means, list all your debt from the most difficult to pay to the easiest one or the most important to the least important so you can have everything on paper – for example, your number one is your car loan with the bank, number two is your first credit card, number three is your second credit card and number four is a loan from a friend. Consider if you have debt with an interest rate of more than 7% because this can be a significant ongoing cost. How you rank your debt will depend on your situation, so you need to decide which one is the biggest priority for you. Create a plan to repay the debt that's at the top of your list as quickly as possible and really put focus on achieving this, even if you have to make certain sacrifices now. And if debt is not your biggest financial problem but rather the lack of capital for big purchases like a house, a wedding etc. focus your time this week on creating a plan to generate savings and perhaps think about starting to invest.

### Week 3: Do a no-spend week

This week, apart from spending for groceries to cook your food (and not eat out in restaurants or get takeaway) and paying your usual monthly bills for water, electricity etc., do not spend money on anything else – no shopping, no coffee, or drinks with friends. With this challenge, we want you to get in the habit of reducing or eliminating unnecessary spending that's just holding you back and challenge your money decisions – do you really need to spend money on alcohol in a bar or can you do another activity with your friends that doesn't cost you money instead? Put everything you save this week against your biggest debt or capital challenge identified in the previous week. The idea is to challenge yourself for just one week and see what you're able to achieve in terms of results. This is not to say that you'll have to be doing this all the time and live this way.

## Week 4: Review your progress

During the last week of the month, review what you've managed to achieve. Think about what was easy and what was difficult, where were you successful and where did you falter. Find ways to be better and plan your spending for next month, especially following what you decided to do to tackle your biggest debt or financial issue right now. Decide if you can do another no-spend week or maybe two and how much more you could save next month. Or if doing an entire week is too much for you, pick one thing you can remove or reduce spending on. See how you feel about making small changes bit by bit and understand which ones motivate you the most to continue going and getting better at your money mastering journey. The ultimate goal is not to sacrifice all the time and lose any joy but to remove the things that are not bringing you anything and focus on the areas which can provide the highest return over time, financially and emotionally.

These activities are meant to get you in the habit of thinking more strategically about how you manage your money in your day-to-day life and get you easy, quick wins. Every week and month, aim to identify small things you can do better because it's the small things that accumulate and ultimately lead to big progress, allowing you to tackle your toughest financial problems. Money mastering is all about continuous planning of what you can improve and taking the appropriate action to achieve it.

Don't forget to celebrate the progress you have made with this challenge and motivate yourself to continue going. Be proud of yourself and drop us a message on our Instagram channel @money.mastering – we'd love to hear about your journey to money mastering.

Good luck! You can do it!

# ABOUT THE AUTHORS

Iliyana and Fhram are two regular people who have spent a lot of time learning about personal finances and how to manage them better, both individually through a lot of ups and downs and then as a married couple as well. Fhram has a background in the military and Iliyana has spent most of her career in the tech industry. They're both passionate about helping others improve their quality of life through sound, financial decisions as well as simple, daily actions to mastering money. In their free time, you'll find them dancing salsa and enjoying time as a family with their daughter.

# SUPPORT THE BOOK

If you liked this book, please share with your friends and family. Spread the word. Help others be in better control of their money through better financial knowledge.

Also, write us a review on Amazon to share your experience with others and help them make the decision to read the book as well.

Follow us on Instagram @money.mastering and subscribe to www.iliyanastareva.com/money-mastering for more content.

# REFERENCES

[i] Naím, M. (2014). Most People in the World Have No Idea How to Manage Their Money. The Atlantic. Available at: https://www.theatlantic.com/international/archive/2014/05/the-danger-of-financial-ignorance-do-you-understand-money/361851/ [Accessed 21 April 2022]

[ii] Petrov. C. (2021). 20+ Incredible Personal Finance Statistics to Know in 2021. (Blog) SpendMeNot. Available at: https://spendmenot.com/blog/personal-finance-statistics/#:~:text=a%20quarter%20of-,Millennials,-have%20a%20basic [Accessed 22 April 2022]

[iii] World Economic Forum (2019). Retirees will outlive their savings by a decade. World Economic Forum. Available at: https://www.weforum.org/agenda/2019/06/retirees-will-outlive-their-savings-by-a-decade/ [Accessed 15 April 2022]

[iv] Federal Reserve (2021). Economic Well-Being of U.S. Households in 2020 - May 2021. Federal Reserve. Available at: https://www.federalreserve.gov/publications/2021-economic-well-being-of-us-households-in-2020-executive-summary.htm [Accessed 21 April 2022]

[v] Schulz, M. (2022). 2022 Credit Card Debt Statistics. (Blog) Lending Tree. Available at: https://www.lendingtree.com/credit-cards/credit-card-debt-statistics/ [Accessed 30 April 2022]

# REFRENCES

[vi] Johnson, A. (2021). The average credit card balance is $5,525. Here's what you need to know. (Blog) Credit Cards. Available at: https://www.creditcards.com/statistics/credit-card-debt-statistics-1276/ [Accessed 30 April 2022]

[vii] Bureau of Consumer Financial Protection (2019). The Consumer Credit Card

Market. (pdf) Bureau of Consumer Financial Protection. Page 57. Available at:

https://files.consumerfinance.gov/f/documents/cfpb_consumer-credit-card-market-report_2019.pdf [Accessed 29 April 2022]

[viii] Breaking The Debt Cycle (2022). My Money Priorities. (Instagram). 9 August 2022. Available at: https://www.instagram.com/p/ChCpeG_DX4A/ [Accessed 21 August 2022]

[ix] Koop. A. (2021). One Year In: Did People Save More or Less During the Pandemic? (Blog) Visual Capitalist. Available at: https://www.visualcapitalist.com/one-year-in-did-people-save-more-or-less-during-the-pandemic/ [Accessed 15 August 2022]

[x] Yam, K. and Keady C. (2015). 10 Facts That Prove Helping Others Is A Key To Achieving Happiness. (Blog) Huffpost. Available at: https://www.huffpost.com/entry/international-day-of-happiness-helping-_n_6905446 [Accessed 16 August 2022]

[xi] Trading Economics (2022). Netherlands Inflation Rate. Trading Economics. Available at: https://tradingeconomics.com/netherlands/inflation-cpi [Accessed 3 May 2022]

[xii] Maverick, J.B. (2022). S&P 500 Average Return. (Blog) Investopedia. Available at:

https://www.investopedia.com/ask/answers/042415/what-average-annual-return-sp-500.asp [Accessed 17 July 2022]

[xiii] Dividend Mantra (2018). Clinical analysis 1. (jpg) Available at: https://www.dividendmantra.com/wp-content/uploads/2018/04/clinicalanalysis1.jpg [Accessed 19 July 2022]

[xiv] Fidelity Investments (2022). Investment growth calculator. Fidelity Investments. Available at: https://www.fidelity.ca/en/growthcalculator/ [Accessed 20 July 2022]

[xv] World Economic Forum (2019). Retirees will outlive their savings by a decade. World Economic Forum. Available at: https://www.weforum.org/agenda/2019/06/retirees-will-outlive-their-savings-by-a-decade/ [Accessed 21 August 2022]

[xvi] World Health Organization (2022). Ageing and Health. World Health Organization. Available at: https://www.who.int/news-room/fact-sheets/detail/ageing-and-health [Accessed 21 August 2022]

[xvii] Yik, H. (2019). Solving the global pension problem. (Blog) World Economic Forum. Available at: https://www.weforum.org/impact/solving-the-global-pension-crisis/ [Accessed 22 August 2022]

[xviii] World Economic Forum (2019). A quarter of Americans have no retirement savings. World Economic Forum. Available at: https://www.weforum.org/agenda/2019/06/a-quarter-of-americans-have-no-retirement-savings/ [Accessed 22 August 2022]